DATE DUE

APR 9 '01			
JUL 15 '02			
JUL 9 '03			

DEMCO 38-296

KAIZEN
STRATEGIES
—— FOR ——
CUSTOMER
CARE

改善

KAI ZEN

change + good

=

improvement

KAIZEN
STRATEGIES
FOR
CUSTOMER
CARE

How to create a powerful
customer-care program
– and make it work

PATRICIA WELLINGTON

PITMAN
PUBLISHING

PITMAN PUBLISHING
128 Long Acre, London WC2E 9AN

A Division of Pearson Professional Limited

First published in Great Britain 1995

© Pearson Professional Limited 1995

British Library Cataloguing in Publication Data
A CIP catalogue record for this book can be obtained
from the British Library.

ISBN 0 273 61472 X

1 3 5 7 9 10 8 6 4 2

Typeset by Northern Phototypesetting Co. Ltd, Bolton
Printed and bound in Great Britain by
Biddles Ltd, Guildford and King's Lynn

*The Publishers' policy is to use paper manufactured
from sustainable forests.*

THE AUTHOR

Patricia Wellington set up and ran her own manufacturing and retailing organization in the late 1970s and then moved into the field of consultancy in 1986. Her specific areas of expertise are customer care, communication skills and business development. Since joining the Europe Japan Centre in 1993 she has added the vital Kaizen element to her leading edge programmes, making them substantially different from, and more successful than, traditional people-centred initiatives. Not only has she worked on consultancy and training assignments within the UK, she has also worked with the UN in Geneva and undertaken projects in South East Asia.

THE EUROPE JAPAN CENTRE

The Europe Japan Centre is part of a major Japanese corporation, the Osaka Gas Group, with offices in Japan, the USA, Singapore and the UK. The Centre uses these international links to help its clients succeed on a global platform by offering them high quality research and human resources and management development expertise. Drawing on the staff's extensive personal experience of business practices around the world, the Centre offers a unique blend of *the best of East and West*.

THE BEST OF EAST AND WEST

The aim of the Europe Japan Centre is to be a major international influence in business.

To achieve this, we must be flexible, pro-active, informed and adaptable, and our core businesses of research, education and development should be delivered to our clients in a unique way by combining the best of East and West.

Our goal is always to be one step ahead, to anticipate the needs of our clients and to fulfil those needs to the very best of our ability.

We are committed to continuously improving everything we do, by developing our people and working together as a team.

This book is for my son Ben

CONTENTS

Part III
UNITING CUSTOMER CARE AND KAIZEN

PREFACE TO THE SERIES

'Kaizen' offers something new to all organizations and to the people in and around those organizations: a philosophy and framework that encourages them continuously to set higher standards of performance and to achieve new goals in terms of customer satisfaction, sales and, ultimately, profit.

Kaizen is not a new concept. Literally, it simply means improvement, and many people when they hear it explained for the first time look relieved and say they have been doing it for years without knowing what it was called. This is not surprising; most people in the West, as well as in the East, have a desire to improve their work, their relationships, their lives, and many try hard to do so. But – in a management sense, improvement and Kaizen are not synonymous: Kaizen offers far more.

It is the intention of this series to explore exactly how Kaizen can offer more to organizations in the West, how it can help them pull step-by-step ahead of their competitors. In doing this, the Europe Japan Centre has unashamedly extended and modified the original Japanese concept of Kaizen, and has sought to combine the strengths of Western organizations with those of Japan. We are talking about Kaizen for the West, not about a slavish imitation of a concept 'not invented here'.

It seems to us that the time is right for this approach. In the increasingly competitive global market, companies are looking for ideas and practices that work, wherever they originate, not so that they can do exactly the same themselves, but so that they can adapt them to suit their own culture. At the same time, the recession in Japan and the questioning of many practices to which Japan's success has been attributed, means that Japan too is looking for new management ideas, and that for the West now to follow Japanese practices without adaptation would make no sense. Underlying the whole series, therefore, is our theme of 'the Best of East and West'.

Our approach to Kaizen focuses very clearly on the people

element; each title is devoted to a group of people who are key to the success of an organization: leaders of the organization (*Kaizen Strategies for Successful Leadership*), the whole workforce (*Kaizen Strategies for Winning Through People*) and customers, be they internal or external (*Kaizen Strategies for Customer Care*).

For people who have looked on Kaizen principally as a set of processes for improving manufacturing, this approach may seem unusual. It is the experience of the Europe Japan Centre, however, that the most vital determinant in achieving lasting and continuous improvement is the attitude and behaviour of people, and that Kaizen strategies cannot work without the commitment of the people putting them into practice. Although most organizations may know this theoretically, their human resources practices, their leadership styles and their attitudes to customers by no means always reflect this knowledge. This series aims to help bridge this gap between theory and practice.

Researchers at the Europe Japan Centre draw on a worldwide network of contacts to locate and analyze the latest human resources and management ideas and trends. Our consultants and trainers combine these new thoughts with the Centre's practical experience in working with companies in the UK and continental Europe, so that our own services too are continuously improved. The awareness sessions, seminars, workshops and consultancy we offer are designed to help organizations of all sizes and types build on their strengths and create new, more effective strategies through their people. This series of books outlines some of our experiences, and brings together examples of the different approaches of organizations around the world.

The focus of the Europe Japan Centre and of these books is not, however, past practice or even current practice. What we are seeking to do is to stimulate thought, to concentrate the thinking of organizations on the future. Kaizen through people is one way of bringing the future closer, of inventing the future you want for your organization. We hope this series will help you do this in your own way, and we hope too that you will let us know of your success.

Chris Patrick
Director, Europe Japan Centre
July 1995

FOREWORD

America. The year 1621. The word *customer* appears in print for the first time anywhere in the world.[1]

Japan. The same year. The Tokugawa Shogunate has begun expelling all foreigners and is shortly to shut Japan's borders to the rest of the world for the next 240 years.

The echos of these two unconnected events nearly 400 years ago and as culturally distant from each other as it is possible to be are the seeds of this book, for the theory and styles of management and customer service which we know in the West were born largely in expansionist America from the 17th Century, and some of the processes and behaviour which we are now coming to value and adopt in Western business are rooted in the culture of 17th-Century isolationist Japan.

Of course, both nations have changed markedly geo-politically, economically, technologically and industrially since then, most notably due to the events of the 20th Century. Now the cross-fertilization of manufacturing ideas and commercial practices, for example, is a feature of their connected (but competitive) relationship.

The latest phase of that relationship began 50 years ago during the Allied occupation following the end of the Second World War. This not only gave Japan revitalizing money and materials, but also new production and management processes. Dr W. Edwards Deming and Dr J.M. Juran, for example, were American contributors of singular importance to Japan's recovery and current reputation for production quality. Combined with the country's innate sense of national identity, Japan willingly and easily learnt, adapted and adopted alien Western practices into its own cultural traditions and made them uniquely its own. Over the past 10 to 15 years the wheel has turned full circle: Statistical Process Control, Total Quality Management, Quality Circles, Kamban, Just-in-Time inventory control – each con-

---

1 '*Made in America*', Bill Bryson.

taining a kernel of Deming's and Juran's wisdom – have been re-exported to the West as either individual disciplines or collectively as components of the umbrella philosophy of Kaizen.

And the flow of ideas back and forth across increasingly transparent commercial (and scientific) borders has continued since, though Kaizen has yet to be adopted successfully in the West in a textbook-pure form – it is always experienced as an amalgam of 'the best from the East with the best from the West', a blend which many Japanese multinationals themselves are now using to temper purest Kaizen, thus making it more acceptable to Japan's younger and more cosmopolitan managers.

This book, then, is not solely about Japanese Kaizen, nor is it only about Western customer care – and least of all is it a textbook on Oriental versus Occidental management strategies and styles. Rather, it is a practical book that draws together these two themes to create an integrated whole which Western business leaders will find understandable and acceptable. It will inform and advise and motivate you to think deeply about creating a knowledge-based workforce, about customer service and about the powerful underpinning force which Kaizen can be to the strength, sustainability and success of a service strategy.

Together, Kaizen and a policy to care for customers are potent symbols of a company's ambition and capacity to develop an internal culture in which resources – including, importantly, the human resource – are developed fully and utilized effectively. As Imai[2] says in his book *Kaizen*, 'A confrontation between (Japanese and Western) cultures (will) be avoided if you acknowledge the fact that Kaizen will succeed or fail in your organization not for reasons of nationality but of mentality.'

The book is divided into three parts. In Part I we examine the fundamental questions. Kaizen is explained sufficiently to understand what it is (Chapter 2); how it is implemented through particular instruments, for example suggestion systems, Statistical Process Control, Process Orientation Management (Chapter 3); and, overall what its role is as the foundation of organizational culture, management

---

2 Masaaki Imai, author of '*Kaizen: the Key to Japan's Competitive Success*' (1986), and Chairman of the Kaizen Institute, has played a major role in promoting Kaizen throughout the world.

and leadership processes, employee involvement, and internal and external relationships. In Chapter 4 the question, 'What makes excellent customer care?' is explained in some detail.

Each of the five Chapters in Part II considers a specific aspects of the Kaizen approach to Customer Care.

These Chapters plus the four in Part I lay down the broad and detailed foundation for a practical guide to developing, implementing and maintaining a culturally-driven customer-care strategy based on Kaizen.

The two Chapters in Part III examine that strategy in terms of planning and implementing its three core strands – the strategy, Kaizen and customer care (Chapter 10); then in Chapter 11 the guide moves onto maintaining and reinforcing the new culture.

Case histories are used throughout to prove and amplify key points, as are tables, simple line diagrams and end-of-chapter Summaries. The fundamental principle which underscores the writing is simplicity; there is no virtue and little grace in making an opaque thesis out of what is intended to be an immediately useful book for busy leaders and decision makers, who need to access the facts quickly and memorably.

ACKNOWLEDGEMENTS

This book is the product of many people's minds and efforts. Each has contributed insight, facts, experience, introductions and personal support during its preparation. My contacts within companies around the world which have already embraced Kaizen have willingly given me time and access to information which has helped me understand and record in these pages the essential difference that Kaizen and a real attitude of caring for customers has made to their corporate success.

The industrialists and business leaders I would particularly like to thank are: Steve Norman, Regional General Manager, Canon (UK) Ltd; Tom Hay, Managing Director, Bard UK Ltd; Ms Emma Lou Brent, President, Phelps County Bank; Ken Lewis, Managing Director, Dutton Engineering; Susumu Mita, Kansai Business Information; and Michael Dettmers, Dettmers Industries Inc.

I want to also thank my immediate colleagues in the Europe Japan Centre: Chris Patrick, Director, who read each draft manuscript and suggested many valuable improvements; Tony Barnes, who distilled his work with hundreds of organizations in the UK and internationally into a set of thoughts about marrying 'the best of East and West'; Miranda Taylor, Researcher, who helped find and distil important sources of information; and Jean Brewer and Christina Bevan who typed the manuscript – some of it more than a few times!

A special note of gratitude to Patrick Forsyth, Steve Highley, Pippa Bourne, and David Senton who have all, in different ways, helped and supported me during the last ten years of my work in consultancy.

Finally, I wish to thank Marek Gitlin, a professional OD and HRD consultant, long-time mentor and friend whose help and contribution whilst writing this book and during many assignments has been invaluable.

Pat Wellington
Europe Japan Centre, London
June 1995

PART I

THE FUNDAMENTAL QUESTIONS

改善

1

WHY
DOES
CUSTOMER
CARE
NEED
KAIZEN?

改

Kaizen has been called the single most powerful philosophy in Japanese management.[3] And better customer service is probably the single most ubiquitous non-financial objective of businesses and agencies of all types in the West. In the twelve months up to June 1994, for example, during a rush in the UK to prove customer responsiveness, government departments, public sector bodies and agencies issued over sixty new or revised *Customer Service Charters*. To this number must be added the scores published by private sector companies, each responding to a popular bandwagon.

So the questions are, do customer charters and many customer-care programmes stir the consumer consciousness any more than if the pages on which they are printed flutter by in the breeze? and can a Kaizen approach to customer care make a difference?

THE CITIZEN'S CHARTER

The results of a survey conducted by NOP for Britain's TUC and published in October 1994 found that the public either ignored John Major's centrepiece Charter, or regarded it as a superficial exercise in public relations. Only one third of the 1,007 people interviewed had seen a copy of the Charter and only one in ten had read any part of it.

The director of the Consumers' Association, Dr John Belshon, said that 'Initiatives like the Charter Mark will quickly lose public confidence if they don't reflect public needs.'

---

3 Masaaki Imai, '*Kaizen*'

Hence this book, for it answers both questions. But, what is my central theme?

CENTRAL THEME

This book starts from the premise that organizations throughout the world are realizing that their success depends largely on the extent to which they can satisfy their customers, whether those customers are the public, other businesses or even other parts of their own business.

At the same time, many conventional customer-care programmes are failing to provide satisfaction. Others provide satisfaction for a time, but do not have the flexibility and vision to go on satisfying the ever-increasing demands of customers.

These are areas where a Kaizen approach can make the vital difference. A Kaizen approach, adapted to suit Western national and business cultures, takes a customer-care strategy way beyond a cheery smile or even a genuine desire to please: it embeds attitudes within an organization. The race to satisfy customers never ends – and neither do the benefits of a Kaizen approach.

What makes customers dissatisfied?

Throughout this book, you will find examples of what companies in different countries are doing to satisfy their customers. Some companies have adopted a Kaizen approach; others have adopted just some aspects of it. Before we turn to these positive strategies, however, it is worthwhile going back to fundamentals and asking what it is that makes customers dissatisfied.

The immediate answers to this question are obvious, so obvious, in fact, that we in the West tend to stop asking it when the resolution to a customer satisfaction problem can be so apparently clear.

However, I suggest that we are not asking the right question – indeed, the right questions – and not often enough. The questions should be, what are *we* doing that makes our customers dissatisfied? and why? And we should keep asking them until we know the answer, not only to the immediate problem, but also the *root* of the problem. It is essential that companies devote time and effort to

改

uncovering and eradicating the *fundamental* cause of every customer dissatisfaction issue.

Here, the Kaizen approach can pay huge dividends. It is based on asking questions with relentless persistence, in order to reveal why the problem that caused the dissatisfaction arose and what can be done, not so much to appease the customer but more to prevent the problems ever recurring. Consider this example:

A customer complains that the quality of a jar of jam is poor.

Using the Kaizen approach, the questioning could proceed like this:

- *Why were poor quality products allowed to leave the processing company?*
- Because the quality control was not good enough.

- *Why wasn't the quality control good enough?*
- Because there was pressure to deliver the goods and there were no alternative supplies.

- *Why were the supplies poor in the first place?*
- Because the suppliers were not sufficiently well-informed about the standards required.

- *Why did the company submit to pressure to deliver?*
- Because short-term profit is seen as more important to the company than quality and customer satisfaction.

The question and answer session would go on until the lowermost cause was revealed. Many other examples illustrate the same process. Take another:

A customer is promised delivery of a car on August 1. She goes to collect the car, but is told it is not available.

In this case there are two immediate causes of customer

dissatisfaction: first, there is no car, and second, she was not told in advance that there would be no car.

- *Why is there no car?*
- Because there was a delay in a shipment leaving the factory.

- *Why was there a delay?*
- Because not enough cars of the type ordered by the customer had been produced.

- *Why not?*
- Because insufficient market research had been conducted to assess demand in this country.

- *Why not?*
- Because the company felt it could rely on its experience from elsewhere.

- *Why was the customer not warned about the delay?*
- Because the factory did not warn the sales office.

- *Why not?*
- Because the production line leader was ill and his replacement did not understand the system.

- *Why not?*
- Lack of training, lack of supervision and lack of commitment.

From this questioning approach, a key point becomes clear: Front-line staff receive the customer complaint, but the ultimate cause of the complaint can lie very deep within the organization.

Thus, some of the real answers to the question, what makes the customer dissatisfied?, include:

- lack of internal communication
- lack of staff motivation and/or staff enablement
- lack of research

- lack of communication with suppliers
- lack of commitment to long-term relationships with customers
- lack of management vision and/or commitment.

All of these problems are dealt with in detail in separate chapters later.

Companies which adopt Kaizen will tend to be better placed than other companies to deal with these problems. A company following Kaizen would (a) set up problem-solving teams to investigate the causes of the problem and come up with answers, and (b) would have in place an environment that minimized the problems outlined above.

Dutton Engineering (Woodside) Ltd, for example, has seen many tangible benefits from its Kaizen programme – not least of all customers who are more satisfied, and more successful in their own right too.

DUTTON ENGINEERING LTD

Dutton Engineering (Woodside) Ltd is a subcontract sheet metal working company, founded in 1972, and currently based at Sandy in Bedfordshire. Through the development of a Total Quality Management Programme (TQM), launched in April 1989, the company moved into partnership sourcing with both suppliers and customers and won the Small Companies Award for Excellence in Bedfordshire in 1992.

Since introducing Kaizen, the company has made substantial savings, with no redundancies, no pay cuts and no short-time working. The first hundred employee-suggested improvements saved the company £160,270 – a major achievement for a company with just 26 employees.

Managing Director, Ken Lewis, has headed many changes throughout the company as part of the Kaizen approach. One of the lessons he learned from a trip to Japan was the importance of trust, not only between team members making a particular product, but also between manufacturers, suppliers and customers.

In his company in the UK, Lewis has worked hard to build trust relations with suppliers and customers. He actively encourages as much contact as possible between manufacturing cells and customers. 'The philosophy used to be to keep customers away from the people on the shop floor because they might drop you in it. Our people spend time in customers' plants learning more about their needs, finding out how they can serve them better. After all, we want our customers to be successful. It's vital we break down the barriers and recognize that we all want the same thing.'

Dutton's success has been recognized recently by the UK Department of Trade and Industry, which awarded it the Wedgwood Trophy in 1994 for its pursuit of excellence.

In the USA, another small business, but this time in the service rather than the manufacturing sector, has taken some of the principles of Kaizen and created a unique approach to customer service.

PHELPS COUNTY BANK

Emma Lou Brent, CEO of the bank, set a goal in the mid-1990s to make her small-town, rural Missouri bank's name known throughout the state. Less than ten years later, she has succeeded beyond her wildest dreams. The bank is increasingly known, not just throughout the state, but nationwide.

Inc. Magazine, the US publication for growing businesses, has recently featured the company prominently across its eight-page spread on 'Total Customer Service.' According to Emma Brent, 'Our major accomplishment is the relationship we have with our customers.' What is the basis of this success?

Although the bank does not refer to Kaizen in its programmes, many of the techniques it has used are Kaizen-based. In 1989, for example, the company set up a formal participation programme through what it called a 'problem-buster' committee. Six employees with diverse roles and approaches were put on the committee to review suggestions or problems employees knew needed to be solved. The committee could also put out 'problem alerts' to solicit employee input.

The problem-buster committee worked so well that it lost much of its value. People became so accustomed to sharing ideas and information that they were discussing and resolving problems before they were ever raised to the committee. The committee had helped employees create the habit of thinking about and resolving problems both individually and in teams. Once that habit was established, it

▶

created an opportunity to develop more extensive means of involvement.

The new system at Phelps has many features: one of the key areas is an employee share-ownership programme. 'Any one of us can make decisions on his or her own to help satisfy the customer. As employee-owners we are more geared to quality customer service,' says an employee-owner.

One specific innovation has been particularly helpful in improving customer service: Error Alert Response (EARS). In 1992, when empowerment was started, management decided that when employees did make important decisions to solve customer problems, other employees needed to know about it. So EARS was created to use e-mail to make this possible. For example, a customer calls to ask why she received an overdue notice. An employee-owner discovers the reason was an early automatic payment drafted from her account due to a holiday weekend. The employee tells the customer what has happened and that the bank will refund the overdraft charge. Now the employee describes what has happened on e-Mail so that other employees can be alert to this issue.

These are just two examples of how companies in the West as well as the East, in services as well as manufacturing, in small as well as large companies, are turning to the Kaizen approach as a powerful means of revitalizing their companies and making a reality of 'the customer is king' cliché. The following chapters will expand on all these areas to show how you can make best use of the philosophy and practices of Kaizen to give your customer-care strategy the fundamental vitality it needs.

Summary

- Many customer-care programmes have failed because they have not been based on fundamental changes. Kaizen provides the framework and tools for these changes.

- A Kaizen approach helps organizations discover the root causes of customer dissatisfaction and provides the systems and attitudes for introducing improvements.

- A Kaizen approach involves everyone in the company, as well as customers, suppliers and shareholders, in improving the business – thus heightening customer satisfaction. The scope of its approach means that the chances of success are greatly increased.

- Kaizen makes customer care a natural and never-ending process.

2

WHAT
IS
KAIZEN?

改

INTRODUCTION

Kaizen translates as *improvement* (from *Kai*, meaning 'change' and *zen*, meaning 'good'). As used to describe a management process and business culture it has come to mean *continual and gradual* improvement – implemented through the active and committed involvement of all a company's employees in what the company does and, more precisely, in the way that things are done. The Kaizen way does not just mean doing things better though; it also aims to achieve such specific outcomes as *muda* – the elimination of waste (wasted time, money, materials, effort), raising quality (of products, service, relationships, personal conduct, employee development), reducing design, manufacture, inventory and distribution costs, and ultimately in creating more satisfied customers.

It was, perhaps, the first holistic 'movement' in business, for in Japanese Kaizen companies* an employee is recruited and developed as a *whole* person, not simply as a 'utilitarian resource'. The importance of employees and teams, their knowledge of and participation in every aspect of the familial company, and the contribution which each employee can – indeed, *should* – make to improve their workplace and what is produced, are, like an obsessiveness with quality and a focus on customers, the planks of the Kaizen way. These inspire, motivate and make cohesive a workforce which consequently pursues common values and goals and produces results greater than the sum of its members' individual contributions.

---

* The term 'Kaizen company' is used in this book as a convenient shorthand to denote a company (in Japan or the West) which has embraced recognizable Kaizen practices. A 'non-Kaizen company' operates on traditional Eastern or Western lines.

'A society in which individuals feel responsible for their actions is more likely to work together and survive to spread its values. A group of free individuals who share certain mutual aims can collaborate to achieve their common objectives and yet still have the flexibility to innovate and find new directions. Thus, such a society is likely to prosper and, notably, other societies and groups are likely to copy their successful culture.'

'A Brief History of Time', Stephen Hawking

KAIZEN'S PRINCIPLES

Kaizen is a way of thinking and behaving. It provides guidelines for individuals and teams in the 'company family' and helps to direct effort towards fulfilment of the overarching remit of profit through product and process improvements designed to enhance customer satisfaction. (Note the intentional order of 'product', 'process' and 'customers' in the remit: Japanese markets have traditionally been product-driven rather than customer-led; Kaizen's primary emphasis on product quality before care quality reflects this.)

Improvement in a Kaizen company is everyone's concern. Every employee is free to consider any initiative which might improve a product, further eliminate waste or push costs down further. A Kaizen group is thus less constrained than, for example, a specific-project group, a quality-control group or an employee in a traditional Western company, who could be reproached for concerning him or herself with issues relating to a function or department other than their own.

EVOLUTION VERSUS REVOLUTION

A key concept within Kaizen is that change is endemic: nothing is static, there is no *status quo*.* Everything is to be reviewed *continuously*. The consequence is that improvements which are imple-

---

* However, this *is* maintained between employees of different rank, between the male population and women, and between customers and customer servers.

mented need not be big – in other words, they can be small, incremental modifications – to ensure that best quality and practice is always current. And during the past 50 years a veritable litany of tiny, evolutionary advances have transformed the Japanese economy and given consumers around the world products which continually set new standards. It is rare today for Japanese companies in many sectors to find themselves in the position of having to perform a *quantum leap* to overtake a Western competitor or regain market position. It is because the Japanese are so adroit at constantly reviewing and improving today's products that they can so regularly and apparently with ease introduce new models: these could well be constructed around the same core components as their predecessors, but they will have been improved – new features, new design, new materials – just sufficiently to excite consumers by their added-value. It is an alien behaviour in a Kaizen company for it to rest on the laurels of this year's product only to do something with it when a competitor steals the laurels away.

Kaizen's evolutionary approach and the quantum leap revolutionary approach can be differentiated by the emphasis placed in Kaizen on, for example, cross-functional collaboration – the use of existing technologies (or products) as the foundation for new commodities, team sharing and comprehensive feedback – which contrasts with the individualism, limited openness and limited sharing that can characterize an archetypal Western approach to creation and innovation.

In Kaizen companies, it is quite usual for ideas for product, service or company improvement to be the prerogative of each *multiskilled* employee: knowing that quantum leaps are not the sought answer, each feels competent to participate fully in the evolution of their organization by contributing only small-step ideas. (However, as technology, materials and consumers' desires are changing so incredibly quickly, Japanese industrial leaders are aware that their people's knowledge could be eclipsed. To prevent this, a number of the industrial giants have established 'blue skies' research laboratories in which creative thinkers are given a 'limitless' budget to actually find the quantum leap that will propel their company far forward. Mazda, for example, opened its £40m 'M2' concept and design studio in Tokyo for just this purpose.)

THE PRINCIPLES

In this book I shall discuss Kaizen's *ten* principles. They are the classic principles of Kaizen as practised in some companies in Japan. Other literature and Kaizen experts might refer to a different number (or none), but this merely reflects the difficulty of reducing a philosophy to a set of prescriptive rules or instructions. Nevertheless, Kaizen companies exhibit very similar traits of management style/process and it is these which are listed below as Kaizen's principles.

It must be remembered that Kaizen in its *pure* form is neither wholly acceptable to Western thinking and behaviour nor entirely virtuous and in the best interests of employees; in fact the Japanese themselves are now introducing Western psychology and business practices to create less individually coercive and group-oriented environments in Kaizen companies, with the aim of giving more personal freedom, stimulating individual initiative and innovation and establishing new personal performance and merit reward systems – in other words, a more *balanced* culture that blends East and West. There is little doubt that the Japanese have embarked on this course in direct response to the 1991 recession, criticisms levelled at the country's business and political leaders in the media and as a consequence of what they have learnt about employee management and motivation in their plants in the UK and USA. I amplify these points in 'Kaizen and the changing Japanese business environment' on page 23. It should also be noted that not all customer care in Japan is a result of Kaizen: some is due to an innate sense of courtesy and respect; some is purely the consequence of overmanning which can result in six waiters serving each table in a restaurant, each performing one small and highly-demarcated function!

1 Focus on customers

Underpinning Kaizen is a long-view focus on customers' needs. It is absolutely paramount in Kaizen that all activities must lead inexorably to greater customer satisfaction. Kaizen permits no middle ground: a company either provides quality products and unmatchable satisfaction through them or it does not. It is *everyone's personal*

改

responsibility in a Kaizen company to ensure its products (and the service to get them into customers' hands) meet customers' needs. (Note that, Kaizen's *primary* focus is product quality, but as there is no distinction between producing quality products and fulfilling customers' needs the quality of service is inextricably bound into the manufacturing-selling chain. My contention is, Kaizen can accommodate customer care in its direct focus also.)

2 Make improvements continuously

Searching for ways to improve does not stop in a Kaizen company once an improvement has been implemented. Each advance will be incorporated in the design/manufacturing/management process as a new and formal *performance standard*. For example, an improvement which reduces the time taken to change the cutting tool on a lathe will be recorded in an operating manual not simply as a new way of setting up the machine but as the timed standard against which a machine operator's personal performance will be judged. However, today's standard will last only as long as it takes another employee or team to find a way of bettering it.

SMED

The 'Single Minute Exchange of Dies'

It took Toyota's employees four hours to change the dies on the company's large sheet metal presses, compared to Volkswagen's employees who could do a comparable job in two hours. That was in 1970, and Shigeo Shingo, a Toyota Team Leader, believed an improvement was possible and necessary.

After six months his team had reduced the set-up time to 1.5 hours; but far from ceasing their search for improvement once the two hour 'target' had been breached, the team continued to bring the time down until they could change the dies within three minutes. (The 'single minute' in SMED means single *digit*.)

The important point to note is the ceaseless drive for improvement: in Kaizen the search for improvement must never stop.

---

3 Acknowledge problems openly

Every company has problems. Kaizen companies are no exception, but by fostering an appropriately supportive, constructive, non-confrontational and non-recriminatory culture it becomes possible for every workteam to bring its problems into the open. Here they can be considered by everyone in the team, department or company and made the subject of resolution ideas from all quarters.

Such openness should be compared with what can happen in closed organizations, where problems are either not admitted or kept hidden. The resolution of these problems will consequently be handled conspiratorially or on the basis of ideas contributed by only an intimate coterie of staff. This excludes the possibility of non-involved others contributing innovative ideas from 'outside the square'.

The Kaizen way undeniably takes management courage to share out the power base and power structures. So does managing a company in which problems are *rumoured* to exist, and in which blame and innuendo cloud corporate vision.

4 Promote openness

There tends to be less functional compartmentalization or ringfencing in a Kaizen company than in a Western counterpart. Similarly, working areas are more open-plan in Japan: only the most senior executives will have individual offices, and the usual symbols of rank or status are rarely seen – communality is favoured; all of which reinforces leadership visibility and communication viability.

5 Create work teams

Each individual in a Kaizen company belongs to a workteam managed by a team leader. In addition, an employee will be associated with a year group (consisting of contemporaries who joined the company at the same time and which confers a level of seniority on its members), plus one or more *ad hoc* or standing Quality Circles and cross-functional project teams. Membership of various overlapping teams – *networking*, in our sense – draws employees into corporate life and reinforces the feeling of mutual ownership, collective responsibility and company-centredness. (*See also* the section on Teams and Team Leadership later in this chapter.)

改

NETWORKING

Networks (electronic or personal) within companies destroy rigid hierarchies and blur the traditional barriers between departments and divisions. They allow workgroups to evolve for the solution of specific problems. The network provides a constantly updated data platform for a company's entire staff to draw on.

In a networked business, leadership becomes more important than management, and command and control is replaced by communication. A network's main characteristic is openness of information. This requires stronger relationships between peers, empowers employees – who can now get whatever information they need to do their job – and raises the key issue of trust.

The *Daily Telegraph Magazine*

---

6 Manage projects through cross-functional teams

Kaizen states that no individual or single-function team will necessarily have all the skills or best ideas to efficiently manage a project, even one concerning its own discipline. The functions which should be represented in a multidiscipline project team from the beginning will be those directly influenced by the project *throughout its life*. In the West, in the motor and aircraft industries especially, this is known as 'simultaneous engineering'. The skill in resourcing a cross-functional team, therefore, is to cast the net as wide as imagination allows. For example, it might be desirable to include at project inception representatives from Personnel, Training, Marketing and Sales in, say, an engineering team tasked with redesigning next year's product. These staff can then make fully-informed operational decisions, correctly revised as the project develops, which concern their own responsibilities, and contribute ideas based on their own perspectives (which could influence the product's design).*

---

* Although cross-functional, teams, simultaneous engineering, are a comparatively recent idea in many Western manufacturing organizations, they have existed in hospitals as 'case teams' for complex surgical procedures for decades. A case team might consist of not only the theatre staff but also the pre- and post-operative nursing and care staff, who would meet to discuss the required processes and resources and plan simultaneously the entire programme of activities before committing the patient to surgery.

善

BOEING

The passenger doors – known as 'plug doors' – on Boeing's 747 are truly design and engineering masterpieces. At the time that the 747 was being planned there was a separate door design team; it liaised with other individual teams, when its work affected theirs. Because the doors are so vital to passenger safety and evacuation the door team became the lead team at a critical moment in the aeroplane's construction; but because the various teams operated in discrete 'functional silos', every alteration in the door specification rippled from the door team to the aircraft skin team, to the airframe team, to the wing team and so on in a knock-on cascade that gathered pace as the ripples spread out. The effect was to add significant time and costs to the door project.

When the latest Boeing aircraft, the 777, was being designed, however, Boeing's work practices were being greatly influenced by the Japanese consortium responsible for fuselage sections. 'Working Together' became the watchword describing the new simultaneous engineering approach to the plane's design and manufacture. The newly-designed plug doors for the 777 – which went into operational service in mid-1995 – are the creation of a cross-functional team, whose members – from the airframe, fuselage, wings, cabin, safety and evacuation, and marketing teams – were involved together from the beginning. (Indeed, the design of the entire aircraft is significant in that Boeing's customers were consulted and involved from the very beginning.) The final door design (again, an engineering masterpiece) was achieved with significant savings in time and cost compared to the expense of the doors on the 747.

7 Nurture the right relationship processes

A prime factor in the Kaizen way is the emphasis on management process; Kaizen companies are just as concerned and driven by the achievement of financial goals as any company, but their premise is: if the processes are sound and relationships are designed to nurture employee fulfilment, then the wanted outcomes will follow inevitably. This principle can be described by one word that carries great weight in Japanese culture: *harmony*. Harmony is most apparent in the Japanese desire for non-adversarial communication and the avoidance of inter-personal confrontation.

改

8 Develop self-discipline

The most observable evidence of Kaizen's roots in Japanese religious and social culture is an employee's self-discipline. Kaizen demands this, not only because allegiance to the workteam and self-controlled behaviour are understood to be part of the natural order but also because respect for one's self and company indicates inner strength and wholeness and a capacity to harmonize with colleagues and customers.

This is the most alien Kaizen principle to Westerners, who in general are less prepared to sacrifice their families and their social time for the company or an individual manager on an on-going basis. And yet, quite clearly there are major benefits to be gained from as many employees as feasible having a sense of self-discipline and determination. However, for those in the West who naturally have a sense of entrepreneurship and creativity there is much to be gained by the enablement/empowerment process.

9 Inform every employee

Kaizen requires all staff to be fully informed about their company, at induction (which in Japanese companies is a *critically* important, formal, structured, comprehensive and lengthy process) and throughout their employment; the point being that the right attitude and behaviour are contingent upon a complete understanding and acceptance of the company's mission, culture, values, plans and practices.

10 Enable every employee

Enabling employees gives them the skill and opportunity to apply the information provided. Through multiskill training, encouragement, decision-making responsibility, access to data sources and budgets, feedback and reward, Kaizen employees are empowered to materially influence their own and their company's affairs. (That said, the degree of individual and team empowerment is strictly bounded in Japan by the limiting effect on personal freedom of centuries of observance of hierarchy and rank. In contrast, Western cultures have historically encouraged individuality, personal initiative, even maverick behaviour; our response to hierarchy and rank has tended to be respect only for those who have earned it rather than acquiring it merely due to age. I believe, therefore, that Western employees can initially find it easier to handle empowerment than their Japanese counterparts and can perhaps exploit it more fully.)

Of these ten principles five (5,6,7,9 and 10) refer to the training and development of people, and it is these five principles which are the most readily transferable into a traditional Western company to establish a Kaizen culture. They compound the energy, commitment and drive of employees and help to create the feeling of an in-company community working together within a larger customer society.

The case of Shimamura Inc., a Japanese discount store company, illustrates several of these principles and shows how part-time employees are considered of equal importance to full-timers.

SHIMAMURA INC.

Shimamura Inc. is a discount store company operating through 266 branches across Japan; it sells mostly women's clothing and household items.

It is different from many companies in its human resources programme, which:

- allows part-time employees the opportunity to take high positions in the company
- encourages the active participation of all employees, whether full- or part-time.

Unusually in Japan, half of the company's shop managers are women.

Part-time employees: the company observes the philosophy that part- and full-time employees are equal. They enjoy the same rates of pay, the same benefits and the same promotion opportunities.

The company believes women are extremely good employees, but as many cannot work full-time their abilities are wasted. Some of the company shops are in areas where it is difficult to find staff; part-timers solve this problem. The company prefers to employ local staff, not specifically because of costs, but because they feel local staff understand local customers best.

▶

改

▶

> **Kaizen:** the company issues a series of five staff manuals which all employees in the stores must know and use: these contain all the information necessary for employees; on products, behaviour, company policy, etc. Unlike in many companies, these manuals are continually changing. All employees are encouraged to make proposals to improve what is in the manuals (and, therefore, in the way the stores operate).
>
> Once a suggestion is made, there is a strict procedure for dealing with it. Suggestions considered useful by the shop managers and senior executives are announced at the monthly meeting held for shop managers. The employee(s) responsible for accepted suggestions is rewarded, and bulletins about the suggestion and person(s) are displayed on notice boards.
>
> **Keeping the momentum going:** The company is very conscious that suggestion schemes often lose momentum. Therefore:
>
> - all suggestions are reacted to within a month
> - good ones are incorporated in the manuals immediately, so staff can see progress occurring all the time
> - those which are not used are returned to the person who suggested them, along with comments and an acknowledgement of the effort and thought contributed.
>
> As a result, between 500 and 800 suggestions per store are submitted each month.

Clearly, empowering employees without controls to contain possible abuses of delegated power and responsibility could be disastrous. Each individual's and team's sphere of influence is therefore bounded in a Kaizen company by strict cultural, behaviour and discipline standards which govern and focus how employees use their initiatives and collaborative efforts.

While at first glance the forces of control might appear quite awesome, they are no more than boundary lines funnelling individual and collective effort towards a particular objective. Self- and intra-team discipline (peer pressure) plus benevolent team leadership are more powerful regulators of behaviour in a Kaizen company than the system of verbal and written disciplining in a Western company. However, the negative view of Kaizen control is coercion to conform and loss of personal autonomy.

KAIZEN CONTROL AND FOCUS

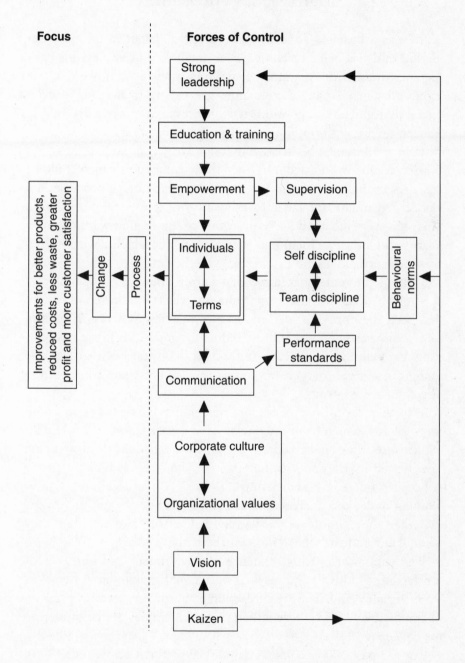

改

KAIZEN AND THE CHANGING JAPANESE BUSINESS ENVIRONMENT

Kaizen as a business concept has evolved in Japan in the post-war period and has been acclaimed as a major key to success in many Japanese industries. At a time when the Japanese economy is in recession and when Japanese companies are having to face up to ever-increasing global competition, it is, however, important to look at Kaizen's place within the whole of Japanese business.

First of all it must be stressed that not every company in Japan is a Kaizen company – far from it. Even those companies which could be called Kaizen companies as far as their manufacturing processes are concerned might not fall into this category if their administration divisions were included. Certain sectors of the economy, for example distribution, despite including some companies which have a Kaizen approach, are, as a whole, extremely inefficient.

It should be remembered too that Kaizen operates in Japan within a wholly different business environment, where lifetime employment has been the norm for men in large companies. Whereas Kaizen in the West has sometimes led to a reduction in jobs, in Japan cost-cutting by making employees redundant has not been acceptable (employees are, however, frequently required to change jobs within the company or group).

A further key difference is that decision making operates on a consensus basis, which from a Western viewpoint is laborious and inefficient; the time necessitated to reach decisions is now being questioned in a number of companies. The overwhelmingly strong emphasis on teams and groups, rather than individuals, is also coming under the microscope, as companies have begun to wonder whether they should reward individual effort and whether they should aim to foster more individual creativity.

The continuing strong influence of government and bureaucracy on Japanese industry and markets means that changes are often slow to materialize and that rapid reaction to events or overseas pressure is impossible. Again, these structures and attitudes are beginning to be challenged.

For the past 50 years Japan has striven to catch up with the West. Now it needs to relax its employment policies, become more flexible and innovative, pay more regard to the psychology of people at work, and strip away the stifling layers of legislative bureaucracy to retain its position as the world's second richest nation. Perhaps there are lessons which the West can teach Japan and its corporate managers at the same time as the West is learning about Japan's successful business management policies. In fact, it might be argued that companies in the West which have blended Kaizen with Western business and employee management theory are *existing* models which the Japanese can emulate.

Change

A number of factors are beginning to (slowly) exert a collective influence on Japan's management culture: the 1993/94 political and financial corruption scandals, the recession during the same period, younger and globally-educated managers, the exchange of ideas between Western firms in Japan and Japanese conglomerates in the West, and the 1995 earthquake have each asserted a certain pressure to change. Companies such as Nissan, Komatsu, NSK, Matsushita, Toshiba and Fuji are responding: they have already seen how a blending of Kaizen with Western management and motivation theory (Maslow, Herzberg, Mayo, McGregor, Blake and Mouton and Argyris, for example) produces more motivated employees and a highly-productive and innovative environment which does not depend on obedience to rank and 'group think' to produce results.

Summing up

It can be readily understood from the brief outline of Kaizen and its ten principles in this Chapter that it is a potent force within organizations. It defines and controls organizational culture, values and the management process. It influences product development and manufacture through an emphasis on continuous improvement, quality control, cost reduction, waste elimination, and manufacturing process and inventory controls (*see* Chapter 3). It governs relations with suppliers and customers. It informs and motivates internal relationships through strong team-leadership, team-centredness, open communication and individual and collective responsibility to review and enhance the totality of work. It oversees employee recruitment,

改

induction and development and encourages participation through information sharing, education, empowerment and activities such as quality circles and cross-functional collaboration.

Overall, Kaizen has a single paramount objective – customer satisfaction through quality products; its principles and instruments are merely the means to this end. In this regard Kaizen makes the significant difference between only those staff in a customer service department bearing the responsibility for customer service (so typical of Western companies) and *every individual employee* understanding the inextricable link between their daily conduct and customers' perceptions of their company and its products. Thus, *everyone* in a Kaizen organization knows they are each customer-facing, and that the responsibility for service is a personal one which cannot be delegated away to another person or a customer-service team.

Yet all this must be balanced by the view that so much about Japanese business administration is horrendously inefficient and quite inappropriate at the end of the industrial 20th Century. If there is one thing that Kaizen has prevented it is *personal* initiative and decisiveness, plus that individual entrepreneurial spark that makes typical Westerners inventive, inquisitive, acquisitive and willing to challenge received wisdom.

We in the West can learn from Japan's paradoxes – we can *go beyond pure Kaizen* – and create a service industry culture that matches Japan's manufacturing culture, by interweaving the management theories that rightly inform our business practices with an adapted Kaizen. The best from the East with the best from the West is the answer. Samsung has already discovered it:

SAMSUNG

South Korea's *gerontocratic* corporate culture – a mirror of Japan's – is feeling the fresh wind of change blowing through Samsung, Korea's largest conglomerate with a product portfolio that ranges from DRAM memory chips to fire insurance. Lee Kun-hee, Chairman since 1992 and still only 43 years old, believes that his staff should have independent lives and interests outside the workplace. His employees start the day early and are positively encouraged to leave by 4pm, an unheard of hour in Far Eastern companies. He has pushed decision making to the lowest levels and expects team leaders and managers to treat employees as human beings rather than robots. Lee says that weary and stressed employees lack attention, initiative and creativity – three qualities he believes are essential to Samsung.

Samsung Electronics was voted the third most admirable company in Asia in 1994.

To develop into a Kaizen company, many changes will be necessary. For most Western companies these will range from structural changes, for example, and most importantly, the active and overt introduction of team-based working, to *attitude* changes that turn Western employees into 'Kaizen people'. I explore this point over the following pages first, by examining Kaizen teams and team leaders and second, by looking at what makes a Kaizen person.

AN EXAMINATION OF KAIZEN TEAMS AND TEAM LEADERS

Team Leadership

In Japan, rank is very important and overtly recognized. In Kaizen companies employees are organized into workteams led by team leaders, and so important are teams in these organizations that individual status is taken from the group status and rank of the team.

In Western terms a Kaizen team leader could well be a supervisor or a manager, but the role is different from that fulfilled by a traditional Western manager or supervisor. A Kaizen team leader will be foremost a coach, communicator, trainer, motivator and a resource which his team can use to intercede with senior management on their behalf for, say, funds to trial an improvement (*see* the section on Kaizen Suggestion Systems in Chapter 3). The team leader will be concerned primarily with 'how' his team works rather than 'what' they produce: remember, one of the tenets of Kaizen is, get the management process right and the wanted outcomes will follow naturally and inevitably.

改

A team leader's typical job description reflects this process-oriented style of management. The most important factor in a leader's job description will be his responsibility for human relations, requiring a knowledge of self and human nature plus skills in leadership, motivation, reconciliation, communication, meetings management and training. A vital responsibility of the team leader is to achieve a constructive balance between the identity and demands of the team (as an organic entity) and the individuality and needs of its members. A team will continue to exist only as long as it continues to share:

- compatible values
- the same vision, mission and goals
- mutual respect, trust and loyalty
- its knowledge and skills
- collective ownership
- belief in the *strength* endowed on it through any internal diversity of character and preference - and only as long as the leader retains the team's respect.

Secondarily in his job description will be the leader's responsibility for quality, improvements and productivity; however, these will be expressed more in terms of his responsibility to encourage *the team* to achieve the quantitative outputs and qualitative standards than in terms of personal production quotas. In other words, a Kaizen team leader focuses his attention on people directly and results indirectly – by and large the inverse of a Western supervisor's job.

Teams

To become a team a group of employees must have a strong common purpose and a desire to work together to satisfy that purpose. One of the most crucial aspects of a team is that it must be capable of achieving results beyond the sum of its members' individual contributions. (It is said that, in Kaizen teams, one plus one equals *three*.)

It should be clear that Kaizen teams are much more than *loose* groups of employees who happen to be neighbours on a production line, around a specific machine, in the same office or performing the same function. Workteams – more so in manufacturing than service or administrative functions – are the very bricks from which the foundation of group life in a Kaizen company is built. Each team will be formalized, individually identifiable and acknowledged as an intimate component of the corporate structure. A team's success will depend on first, the extent to which its purpose is clear and homogeneous and second, the degree to which it is enabled. This means that significant amounts of information from the company must be made available, and that the team must be motivated, educated and given the necessary autonomy. It too must be controlled by adequate checks and balances on performance. In this way, Kaizen teams can behave like mini-companies.

The true extent to which individuals and teams can contribute positively is frequently undervalued – even managed *out* – in Western companies (despite the theories from Herzberg, McGregor, et al). The most emancipated organizations have long understood this and therefore created a dynamic environment of considerable team-autonomy based on extensive and profound personal transformation education.

SONY

The Sony project team which developed the Data Discman was empowered by a unique set of nine operational principles:

1 The first priority is to decide what size the product should be, even before considering what it should consist of.
2 Believe everything can be half the size initially thought the minimum.
3 The target must be clear and simple.
4 You must agree the target unanimously and motivate yourself for success before considering the detailed substance of the project (or product).
5 'Difficult' means possible; 'impossible' should be excluded from your discussions.
6 Before explaining (or attempting to explain the idea) make the product.
7 Brainstorm in your hotel; do not end your discussions or return to work before your target is reached.

▶

改

8 The most promising ideas or products must be kept secret from your boss; you must make the product before telling him.
9 If you want assistance ask the busiest people: they are the ones who will have the best ideas.

Source: Simon Collinson, Institute for Japanese–European Technology Studies, University of Edinburgh, in *Technology Analysis and Strategic Management*, Vol. 5, No. 3, 1993

Team Meetings

It is difficult to underestimate the importance of team meetings in Kaizen, and of providing time and space for them. However, a Kaizen team meeting is likely to be quite different from one in a Western company: in the worst case these can be long, convoluted, less than wholly participative, convened in less than ideal surroundings and terminally pointless.

In Kaizen, team meetings are an inseparable part of the process of working. They are therefore financially fully justifiable. They actively promote team identity (to members and others), help schedule and allocate team resources at, say, the beginning of a shift, and provide a necessary forum in which production standards or problems, individual needs, lessons that have been learnt, improvement suggestions or company information can be aired and shared. They are a vehicle by which the team leader can be seen to be exercising his or her communication and interaction skills, and by which the ability to achieve full participation in a consultative and consensus process can be judged: Kaizen team meetings are most definitely two-way! To continue the analogy of teams being the foundation bricks of corporate structure, team meetings are the mortar which binds work into a cohesive and homogeneous whole.

Time

Commonly, team meetings will be brief and focus on only one or two specific objectives: a half-hour meeting at the beginning of, or early into a shift, is typical, as is an hour per week to, for example, discuss improvement suggestions, performance or personal development. Longer or more frequent meetings might be necessary at the start or towards the end of a project; but in any event, meetings are not seen as an interruption of everyday work: they *are* an everyday and necessary part of team-based working, and in Kaizen companies quite unremarkable for that.

Venue

The venue for a team meeting can significantly influence the quality of its outcomes. In Kaizen companies, therefore, venues can be more than merely empty offices; in their colour, lighting and facilities they not only support the working aims of meetings they should also promote harmony, reflection and creativity. In factories in Japan it is not uncommon to find a purpose-designed meeting room or 'corner' for each team in a Kaizen company.

THE 'KAIZEN PERSON'

Although the Kaizen approach traditionally focuses on the importance of teams and team work, Kaizen adapted for the West aims to blend the positive aspects of individualism with the advantages of team work. Companies such as Nissan in the UK have shown how powerful this blend can be.

Whilst it is vital not to crush creativity by imposing rigid standards, the following description of the 'Kaizen person' may be helpful in focusing attention on the behavioural attributes which are particularly useful in implementing Kaizen. A 'Kaizen person' shows:

- attention to detail
- a forward-looking approach
- receptivity to constructive advice
- willingness to take responsibility
- pride in his or her work and organisation
- a willingness to co-operate.

改

Summary

- Kaizen means continuous and gradual improvement.

- Kaizen's ten principles are:

  1 Focus on customers.
  2 Make improvements unceasingly.
  3 Acknowledge problems openly.
  4 Promote openness.
  5 Create work teams.
  6 Manage projects cross-functionally.
  7 Nurture supportive relationship processes.
  8 Develop self-discipline.
  9 Inform every employee.
  10 Enable every employee.

- Kaizen is a powerful and unifying force. It should be the goal of a company wanting a change in organizational culture and style as the strategic precursor to a customer-service programme. This will differentiate the programme from a superficial exercise in public relations.

- For Western companies, Kaizen needs to be blended with Western management theories to create an accepted and employee-endorsed working environment.

- Kaizen does not depend on specialist groups (as Total Quality Management (TQM) can), but on every employee individually.

- Kaizen team leaders are appointed on the strength of their motivating, communicating and training abilities.

- Teams are the essential building blocks of corporate structure in Kaizen companies.

- Team meetings are brief, focused, participatory and a vital part of the two-way management process.

- No topic is considered exclusively either someone else's responsibility or entirely one's own. Improvement ideas can be offered by anyone at any time and concern any part of the entire production/administration/service operation.

- 'Kaizen needs employees who are encouraged to think and trained to think critically and constructively. This requires the right corporate culture and values. The Kaizen way is a reason for continuous training: the more knowledge and skill a workforce has – the deeper and wider the skills pool – and the more it is empowered, the better will be the quality of improvement to products and customer service.'   *Kaizen for Europe*, R.Hannam (IFS Ltd, 1993)

As John Guaspari, a vice-president of Rath and Strong, an American management consultancy, has said, 'the significant gap that can exist between attitude and action may in part be attributed to the fact that many employees are not taught how their work impacts upon the level of value that customers receive.'

3

WHAT
ARE
KAIZEN'S
INSTRUMENTS?

改

INTRODUCTION

I use the word 'instrument' to mean a specific production process or management tool based on one or more of Kaizen's principles and used in the context of a Kaizen culture. Many instruments which help in the implementation of Kaizen are already used in Western organizations. Some of the following could therefore be familiar.

However, taking one Kaizen instrument, Just-in-Time (JIT) inventory control, as an example of what has happened to Kaizen-based activities when they are used out of context, it is apparent that some Western organizations have misunderstood the purpose of, and the part that employees play in, Kaizen's instruments. The tendency was to employ an instrument as an end in itself; in other words, JIT became the goal but for internal reasons only. Of course, there is nothing inherently wrong in that – after all, reducing stock-holding costs and thereby improving cashflow (two of JIT's benefits) are ways of increasing net profit. Nonetheless, two elements of the full Kaizen 'equation' were often ignored: first, a Kaizen instrument should not be an end in itself – it should be a means to improving production to provide greater customer satisfaction. This is the real goal, but it was not always the case that managers and employees understood the connection between the installation of a new system (JIT) and its benefits to customers. Second, any Kaizen instrument will fail to achieve its total potential if it is used by only selected staff or departments: quality control, before the advent of TQM, is an example of how companies in the West ringfenced this function within a special department. Quality Circles are another example of an activity in which only some employees were invited to participate; and it is the same in customer service: an attitude that can still be heard today is, 'I work in the factory. The people in Customer Services look after customers.'

In Kaizen companies the management processes and corporate values provide the contextual culture which spells out unequivocally the ultimate purpose of Kaizen's instruments, and by which every employee acknowledges their individual responsibility for quality and service, etc. Thus the Kaizen 'equation' is completed: *context – instrument's end purpose – individual responsibility*. A coherent scheme, as shown in the diagram.

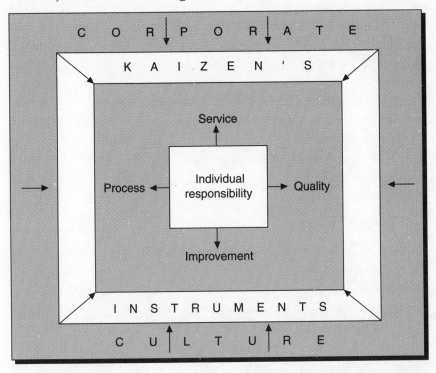

The following, then, are some of Kaizen's instruments. Each, except Suggestion Systems (looked at first), is discussed only briefly merely to explain its key points. Suggestion Systems are discussed more fully because they represent in microcosm the strengths and weaknesses of the Kaizen approach to customers, enablement, inclusivity and group-consensus management.

改

SUGGESTION SYSTEMS

The Western Process

Consider first the bare facts of a typical Western suggestion scheme. (Note the use of 'scheme' in the West and 'system' in Kaizen: similar they may be, but the implied difference between the two processes is significant.) An employee or a group of employees will submit an idea, most probably concerning their own work and probably via a special form which reaches a distant vetting committee by internal post or collection from a suggestions box. The committee members will assess the idea, using functional specialists if necessary to guide them. The assessment will likely cover the idea's viability, the costs of implementing it and any consequent savings to the company. The committee of assessors will decide whether the idea should be taken further. Ideas which have merit might then be implemented either without further refinement or following more development by the originator(s) and/or others. Ultimately, the originator(s) of an implemented idea will be rewarded financially (in the form of an ex-gratia cheque or royalties from patent ownership). The originators of ideas which do not pass the committee screening go unrewarded, even unacknowledged.

The Kaizen Process

A Kaizen suggestion system operates differently. An employee who has an improvement idea concerning any part of their company will first present it to his or her own workteam. They will assess the idea, brainstorming refinements and discussing its potential benefits, with the originator participating fully throughout. But from this early stage the idea passes from individual to team ownership, though the originator will not be disregarded as he or she could be asked by the team to lead the planning project which will evolve from an idea the team agrees has merit. The workteam will be responsible for preparing a business/implementation proposal, using as necessary advice from other workteams and individual employees with specialist knowledge or skills. The proposal will include a cost-benefit analysis clearly indicating *how the idea will improve customer satisfaction*.

(The real indicator of the value of an improvement is the reaction of customers.) Once the proposal is ready it will be presented to the team's leader and then the leaders of any other teams whose work would be affected if the idea were implemented. The team leader(s) will then decide whether to present the idea to their immediate managers who, in turn, will discuss the idea's merit and, if appropriate, seek a release of funds from senior management for a trial of the idea. It will be the team's responsibility to manage the trial and, if it is successful, see it through to full adoption. A key question during the idea's consensus assessment is, does it lead to a new performance standard? If all it amounts to is a different methodology it is not an improvement, nothing will have changed and customers will not be served any better than before. An idea must create a new performance standard (in, for example, lower waste, lower cost, greater speed, etc.).

Not only will the originator(s) – that is, the *workteam(s)* – of an implemented idea be rewarded with morale-boosting recognition, the originators of failed ideas will also be rewarded, for in Kaizen it is important to acknowledge the effort behind *every* suggested idea whether or not it ever sees the light of day. In fact, each team's and team leader's performance is judged partly on the sheer number of improvement suggestions generated in a given period. That only a comparatively few of the contributed ideas are implemented does not matter; the point is, everyone should participate in their company's life. Kaizen's team-based ethos is obvious in the way its suggestion system operates, as are the awareness and competencies of all employees generally who can identify a potential improvement even within functions beyond their own.

改

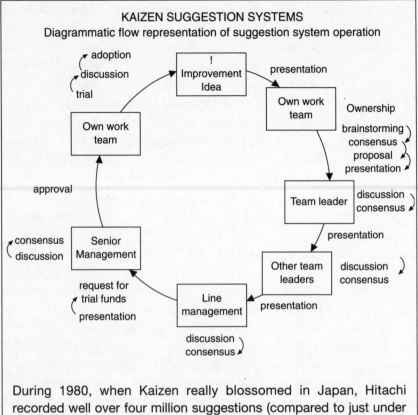

KAIZEN SUGGESTION SYSTEMS
Diagrammatic flow representation of suggestion system operation

During 1980, when Kaizen really blossomed in Japan, Hitachi recorded well over four million suggestions (compared to just under three million the year before). In the same year, Ford recorded 50,000 suggestions. *Active* ideas people in Japan will today submit up to 1000 improvement ideas a year, though the general population of employees will each submit between 20 and 50 ideas per year.

Kaizen's other instruments include:

Quality (Control) Circles

In 1950 Dr Deming delivered the first of his lectures on statistical control and the use of control charts and sampling for quality-checking to the Union of Japanese Scientists and Engineers. In 1951, the Union honoured his contribution by creating the *Deming Award* for institutions and companies which successfully adopted his ideas. By 1960, and building on Dr Juran's 1954 idea that quality should be the responsibility of all employees – from the CEO to the shopfloor – the Japanese government made quality an issue within its national strategy for recovery. By 1962 Japan had fully evolved Quality Control Circles (QC Circles).

These were originally *ad hoc* groups of volunteers led by a senior shopfloor employee whose task was purely to resolve local quality problems as part of the countrywide pursuit of the national quality goal. As the number of problems grew less and recovery was substantially underway – it took little more than the ten years from 1962 to 1972 for the Japanese to gain control over their quality and production problems – each QC Circle developed into a Kaizen group, still voluntary but with the additional much wider remit of finding process improvements. And these are the functions of QC Circles in Japan today; the term *Quality* Circle is a carryover from the 1960s and no longer fully describes the breadth of horizon over which these groups cast their attention.

What QC Circles of course do is keep quality and improvement issues (a) within the domain of all employees and (b) a human-centred process.*

Process-oriented Management (POM)

Whereas traditional Western managers focus principally on results – and each is judged on their 'raw' achievement ('I want those results and I don't care how you do it, just get me them!') – Kaizen managers/team leaders are overtly oriented towards the *process* of achieving the required results. Each is judged therefore by such people-centred skills as ability to encourage team members' involvement, the management of tasks/time, education and training, intrateam participation and team performance (including the number of improvement suggestions generated), morale boosting, communicating, and satisfying customers.

---

* There are several organizations in Japan which promote QC Circles, Kaizen, Small Group Activities (SGA), Suggestion Systems and Zero Defect (ZD) interests. According to the Nihon Gijutsu Remmei, which administers the Deming Award contest, most QC Circles in general work on two or three themes a year, though in rare cases it has been known for some circles to handle up to eight major QC issues in a single year.

改

Expansion of QC Circles in Japan

1950s   Materials industry
            Electricals industry

1960s   Automobile manufacturers

1970s   Auto-parts manufacturers

1980s   Service industries
            (Supermarkets, department stores, hotels, banks)

1990s   Insurance companies, fast-food outlets, small retailers eg
            bookshops

In the USA, QC Circles were first adopted within the service industries, and their spread through hospitals, schools, banks and airlines means that in some service sectors American understanding and use of QC Circles is far more advanced than in Japan.

Visible Management

This is the consequence of POM. When team leaders involve themselves, as is required by Kaizen, in openly instructing and developing their team's knowledge and skills, they are said to be visible. Visible management helps employees to maximize their productivity and holistic qualities.

Cross-functional Management (CFM)

CFM is a *formal* part of fulfilling business plans, strategies and projects in Kaizen companies. There is more than a simple expectation that workteams will collaborate across functional divides, it is a requirement. This eliminates 'problem myopia' and horizons that are artificially narrowed by compartmentalization or territoriality. (*See also* Chapter 5, Breaking Down Internal Barriers).

Just-in-Time Management (JIT)

JIT is the production system developed by Taiichi Ohno at Toyota. It is a pull-through production scheduling and inventory control system. Its aims are broadly threefold: first, to eliminate the waste associated with any activity which does not add value (for example, stock held in a warehouse does nothing and earns nothing and therefore gains no value from being there); second, to reduce (or eliminate) expensive stock piles; third, to ensure that whenever and wherever stock is required it will be available immediately prior to its use, ie 'just in time'. Clearly, a system which depends for its success on a well-timed flow of units into a production area, thence onto and down a production line and finally into packaging and despatch to the point of sale must be regulated with great precision. This can be done by either a substantial and expensive computer programme proactively dictating the speed of an assembly line or the movement of units up and down the entire supply chain (rather than reacting to movements downstream only), or by a manual control system.

Kanban

At its simplest, Kanban is a manual-production scheduling technique controlled by a process operator or machine operator. When an operator comes towards the end of the buffer stock of units he/she draws from his/her immediate work he/she will pass a Kanban card (simply, a reorder card) to another operator upstream of him/her on the production line or in the supply chain. This operator then fulfils the Kanban order from his or her own buffer stock or work-in-progress until he/she also begins to run out of units. He/she will then take his own Kanban card still further upstream. (Kanban cards are now bar coded to eliminate the physical transfer of cards from hand to hand.)

Thus, a sequence of Kanbans moves upstream whenever items are required from a supplier, and downstream with the stock of finished items. Production is thus controlled or pulled-through by demand, often originating from the end-user customer. An example of this can be seen in many high-street retail outlets where bar coded reorder Kanban cards are hung behind the penultimate items on a display rack. When a card shows, a store assistant takes it to an interactive cash register, reads the bar code into it and so triggers a response the length of the supply chain. (This is an example of how a Kaizen instrument ultimately and directly benefits customers.)

改

HONDA

Honda have given the responsibility for determining assembly-line speed to the line **employees** (thus taking it away from management and an inanimate computer programme.) To overcome unequal work rates buffer stocks are held between neighbouring employees. These effectively divide the line into individual work stations. Downstream buffers are replenished by upstream **employees** – using the Kanban system – allowing each employee the freedom to start and stop his line station according to the speed he or she draws units from his/her buffer stock. Overall, the line is controlled by dealers' orders.

PARKER KNOLL

Since Cornwell Parker Furniture, makers of Parker Knoll (and G-Plan) furniture, began *de*-automating the first of its three Buckinghamshire factories early in 1992, it has boosted production by 20 per cent and reduced errors to zero. Order lead times have also been reduced, from 12 weeks to just over 2 days.

Parker used to monitor the movement of nearly 2000 separate furniture components via a Local Area Network (LAN) of 15 shop-floor computer terminals. These have been replaced by a manual Kanban system.

A Kanban marker is placed in each stockpile of components. When the level drops to reveal the marker it is taken up-stream to trigger a fresh supply.

McDonald's serving staff also use the same simple Kanban system to signal to the cooks the time when new burgers are needed.

Statistical Process Control (SPC)

Deming was an academic statistician. The popularity of his SPC in the United States, where he introduced it first, waned only for it to be adopted quickly by the Japanese following his lectures there in the 1950s. Its appeal in Japan was in its message that quality was everyone's responsibility (not just that of a specialist quality department) and that, quality should *not* be targeted like sales, because (a) targets are manipulated and (b) a target confers an upper ceiling on quality. He said that quality must be improved continuously without limit and without attracting an attitude that improvement can stop once a target has been reached.

SPC is based on relatively simple fundamental principles, though the form of analysis is somewhat complex and outside the scope of this book. SPC says that products leaving any production process can exhibit two types of variation to their design specification. The first is inherent in the process and, assuming that the process is capable of reproducing the specification, should not create a product outside specification tolerances. These variations are called 'natural' or 'unassigned', because there is no identifiable or specific cause of them. The second type of variation, called 'assigned' variations, are due to specific causes, for example a worn cutting tool or a misadjusted machine. SPC involves machine operators periodically sampling their own outputs and producing a chart which, using elementary probability theory, helps him or her to decide when to shut down the machine *before* it produces products which fall outside the natural variation tolerance. Each operator is thus intimately and personally involved in the process of measuring and controlling quality.

The PDCA Cycle

This, like each Kaizen instrument, is a simple but powerful tool, in this case for solving problems. The PDCA cycle is an endless improvement cycle in which teams:

Plan (look forward, identify, understand),

Do (appropriate and relevant action),

Check (monitor and evaluate effects, evaluate),

Act (promote feedback to upstream teams).

At each stage action is consolidated, standardised and built into ongoing systems. The next PDCA cycle then takes place.

Other Tools in the Kaizen Toolbox

Many statistical and group techniques can be useful in the daily

改

implementation of Kaizen. Organizations which have introduced Kaizen spend time training employees in a range of skills which help them to put Kaizen into practice. In addition to the undervalued technique of brainstorming, these include:

- process mapping
- fishbone analysis
- Pareto analysis
- histograms
- scatter diagrams
- check lists (tick charts).

Kaizen's instruments are first and foremost human-level systems; that is, none of them needs or relies upon expensive computer hardware and software to achieve perfect implementation and its aims. What they do need, however, is a honed sense of individual responsibility, multifunctional teams, group sharing, strong and benevolent leadership, efficient communication and goal focus. It is this simplicity which enables everyone in a Kaizen company to feel part of their company and to contribute to the achievement of its mission. Neither the highest nor lowest employee need be separated from direct involvement due to, for example, 'technophobia' or the attitude 'But my job doesn't include ... .'

All Kaizen's instruments work well because they are based on relationships – expressed as involvement, trust and responsibility – between people inside and outside the company. However, they do need the right contextual organizational culture to support them: it is fairly pointless introducing QC Circles, for example, into an organization whose culture is still wholly conventionally Western. But if the American armed forces can turn to QC Circles as a means of improving their administrative and executive functions, and JIT in Toyota can be initiated with great success using simple Kanban cards, then surely there are lessons here which other organizations can build on to improve their responsiveness to customers?

This is the question which will be answered in the following Chapters.

Summary

It would be wrong to assume that Kaizen's instruments are appropriate for manufacturing companies or production disciplines only, though these are the functions for which they were evolved. Kaizen can be a universal philosophy applicable to large and small companies, manufacturing and service companies, Japanese and Western companies, new and established companies, sole and group companies. It holds customer satisfaction through product quality in primacy, and even when adapted to a Western business culture – as it must be – it remains a powerful but undramatic way of harnessing contributions from everyone to create openness, harmony, cohesion, strength and, above all, improvement.

- To deliver its full potential a Kaizen instrument must be used within a supporting culture: cross-functional management, for example, becomes a significantly more powerful process when it is a part of a corporate ethos and not merely an intermittent or temporarily expedient activity.

- Similarly, singling out particular employees and making them exclusively responsible for, say, quality or customer satisfaction, by definition excludes others from accepting and living their responsibility for achieving these cultural and value goals.

- Quality or customer satisfaction 'targets' are anathema to Kaizen; a 'performance standard' is the preferred term, but a standard must be wholly transient: it should last only as long as it takes another employee or team to better it. No standard is for ever, and every standard can be improved.

- All Kaizen's instruments are human-centred. This means they can be understood and followed by every employee, without special skills or intelligence. In Kaizen, simple is best.

- Each instrument should be both a symbol of Kaizen and a 'signpost' directing personal conduct and group behaviour towards the fulfilment of customer satisfaction. (Note, however, that not every instrument is directly relevant in a service industry or appropriate to achieving a service goal such as better customer care. SPC, for example, is difficult to apply in an office environment. Of the

改

instruments mentioned here, the following *are* relevant to the achievement of improved customer satisfaction: Suggestion Systems, QC Circles (or Kaizen Groups – the successor to QC Circles), POM, Cross-functional Management and the PDCA Cycle.)

4

WHAT
MAKES
EXCELLENT
CUSTOMER
CARE?

己又

INTRODUCTION

In Japan, 'the customer is god' is the sentiment which underpins the best companies' customer-care strategies. How does this compare with the West? What exactly makes excellent customer care?

In the West, customer care has become what one CEO called the 'discipline of the decade.' Since British Airways' *Putting the Customer First* programme – considered by some to be the forerunner of all contemporary customer service and culture change initiatives in the UK (though it evolved from an initiative in Scandinavian Airline Systems) – the need to be more sensitive and responsive to customers was first acknowledged then acted upon by an increasing number of organizations representing between them every industry and profession from banking to ship building, from leisure to government, from transport to healthcare.

But to what extent is the investment in customer service producing a real pay-back for these organizations, as intended? Many customers are no longer seduced by the window dressing of some customer-service programmes. Customers have become so aware of what has been done apparently in their name that their threshold of service expectation has been raised beyond being grateful for mere surface display. This at least tells us how ubiquitous care programmes are; yet paralleling the ever-increasing expectations seems to be a growing scepticism that they, customers, are the actual beneficiaries: it can seem that 'greater efficiency' is a euphemism for shareholder, rather than customer, satisfaction. Research (*see*, for example, 'The Customer is Key') suggests that what customers want now is depth – substance –

to the service they are promised; a feeling of complete comfort and delight that comes from more than superficialities; a feeling that what they see is not a veneer but the wood from which the whole company is cut.

The adoption of Kaizen throughout a company can fulfill this customer desire. In a Kaizen company excellent customer care is a natural outcome of daily and long-term practices, not a bolted-on extra. Kaizen can minimize causes of customer dissatisfaction, lead to positive 'delight' and, ultimately, to greater customer loyalty.

Elements and Excellence

A company's product or service consists of a number of individual elements, which separately and collectively directly influence customer satisfaction. Between them, the elements – known as the Satisfaction Elements – represent every aspect in the factory-to-outlet cycle. The entire company is thus represented in them. This therefore suggests that it is not *solely* a product's quality nor *solely* a sales person's manner – though these are obvious and tangible influences of customer satisfaction – that create the feeling of complete satisfaction (or dissatisfaction). It also suggests that employees other than those in Sales are involved in the whole process of delivering customer care. In other words, it could be argued that if the provision of, say, an after-sales service was the *only* arbiter of customer satisfaction then the employees in every function except those in the after-sales department could ignore customer service, leaving it to the after-sales team. Similarly, if the customer-services team was the sole arbiter of customer delight then, again, everyone else could leave customer care to them.

Of course, it is not like this in the real world. Given that the Satisfaction Elements represent every company aspect, and given that each element plays a direct part in influencing customer satisfaction, then by definition *every* employee must be(come) involved in some direct way in their company's delivery of customer care. This concept – of *universal* responsibility for customer satisfaction – underscores Kaizen, and also underlines my argument that a Kaizen foundation can help everyone to feel responsible for customer care.

THE SATISFACTION ELEMENTS

What are the elements to which I have referred? There are six, of which the Culture Element is the most influential for it is the origin of the values and belief systems that determine whom the company will serve – its directors, its shareholders or its customers.

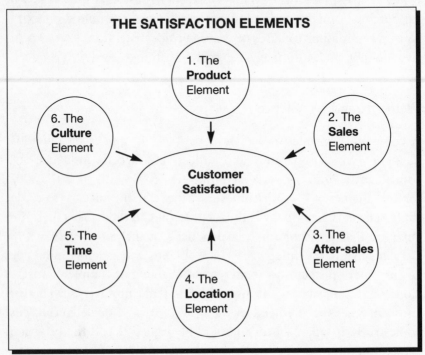

THE SATISFACTION ELEMENTS

1. The **Product** Element

2. The **Sales** Element

6. The **Culture** Element

Customer Satisfaction

5. The **Time** Element

3. The **After-sales** Element

4. The **Location** Element

Each Element can be subdivided into a number of Factors. These more precisely describe the scope of each Element, and the considerations customers bear in mind when choosing one supplier over another. Having said that, not every Factor is consciously considered at every purchase: the psychological/emotional needs a customer experiences when buying a capital expense product (a house, a car, a dining-room suite, a battleship, a combine harvester) will be different from those when buying an everyday or commonplace product (a loaf of bread, cosmetics, an electric kettle, petrol for the car, a book). Nonetheless, even a rapid glance through all the Factors should clearly indicate that much more than the product or the sales person can be considered by customers – business or retail – if they compare the *total* offering provided by each competing supplier.

SATISFACTION ELEMENTS AND STANDARDS OF EXCELLENCE

Satisfaction Element (1) Product

Factor	Excellence is:
Availability	Immediate availability or before a negotiated/promised delivery date (Overall, excellence here is a high speed-to-market time)
Quality	'Lifetime' zero defects
Presentation	Using packaging consistent with the most responsible current environmental-protection standards, and the *minimum* necessary for hygiene/protection/transportation/storage
Image	An image which matches reality, and is fully resonant with the lifestyle and aspirations of target customers
*Value for money**	Ensuring no deception; that is, giving greater (perceived or actual) value than the cost of the purchase
Fulfilment of expectations	Giving satisfaction in excess of expectations

---

*Dr Karl Albrecht, chairman of the Chicago-based TQS Group, has defined value for money as the perceived worth in each customer's mind of the experienced outcome from a business transaction. He has gone on to define what he calls *joint value creation*: value for the customer, value for the organization and value for employees from each transaction.

改

COCA-COLA

Take, for example, the drink Coca-Cola. Its consumers' **needs** are thoroughly and continuously researched to the extent that the company knows more about its target populations' lifestyle, leisure and career ambitions than possibly any other company (though it admits it committed an error of judgement when it launched New Coke in response to what its consumer research correctly showed was a widespread and growing trend towards favouring foods and drinks with less sugar and more natural ingredients. What the research did not indicate was that however much other recipes should be altered the taste of Coca-Cola is as sacrosanct as the design of the Stars and Stripes and not to be tampered with). It is **available** in 185 countries worldwide, and is the most universally recognized brand name on earth. It delivers its promised **benefits** (though these have been considerably toned down from an early claim that, 'this intellectual beverage.... (is) a valuable brain tonic and cure for all nervous afflictions – sick headache, neuralgia, hysteria, melancholy ...'!). It is presented in a **choice** of flavours (eg Classic Coke, Diet Coke), and its **quality** is purer than the general water supply in some of the nations in which it is sold. Its **presentation** is instantly recognizable irrespective of the language printed on its famous hobble-skirt bottle or its recyclable cans. Its associated **images** (health, fun, youth, summer, success, wholesomeness) are promoted heavily (the company's annual advertising and marketing spend worldwide is around $4 billion.) Its **price** is highly variable – in the UK in the summer of 1994, for example, I could pay anything from 24p in a supermarket to 95p from a London street vendor for a can of Coke – yet its **perceived value for money** is invariably high. Needless to say, just about everyone is **familiar** with Coca-Cola: there is nil purchase risk; and consumers' **expectations are fulfilled** – what is expected is delivered time after time.

And yet, its market share is constantly under successful attack by its great rival, Pepsi, and in the UK by newcomers such as Virgin Cola and Sainsbury's own brand of cola drink; even Dr Pepper is gaining popularity, though not necessarily at Coke's expense. Which of the Satisfaction Elements, then, is the Coca-Cola company failing to deliver, given that its Product Element is so nearly perfect?

Satisfaction Element (2) Sales

Factor	Excellence is:
Marketing and Merchandising	Honest, legal and decent marketing that is non-intrusive, non-manipulative and non-wasteful, but informative and targeted precisely in terms of market segment and time; researching customers fully so that their needs, preferences and buyer values are understood in fine detail and incorporated into promotion and business strategies with great accuracy
Verbal communication	A face-to-face or telephone manner that is attentive, interested, responsive and timely, and which conveys an exact and understandable message which meets the customer's objectives and need to be heard; offering different means of placing an order (telephone, fax, letter, personal visit)
Purchase environment	A wholly welcoming and non-threatening environment that is conducive to the easy conduct of business and to making customers feel comfortable emotionally
Staff	Employees who are non-dismissive, responsive, empathetic, trustworthy, knowledgeable, loyal to the corporate team, trained and empowered to act; and whose personal appearance (including the cleanliness and completeness of any uniform) is consistent with customers' expectations
Documentation	Brochures, proposals, estimates, contracts, invoices, delivery notes, training manuals/user manuals, etc. written in *plain* and precise English (and

改

other languages, if appropriate), which *each* includes full company reference/helpline details and which are each accurate and timely

Purchase variables

Explaining them clearly, negotiating them fairly and confirming them in writing

---

T AND K DOUBLE GLAZING

Consider, for example, my own experience of shopping for double glazing. The **product and corporate literature** provided by each company I approached was uniformly of a very high quality – explicit, fact-filled, written for customers like me, and plentiful. All the companies offered some sort of showroom display (from a high-street store to a room set aside in a factory) to see and touch the different product materials and styles, and which surrounded me with a dedicated **purchase environment**. The sales staff I met were mostly knowledgeable and highly-skilled sales closers; they each made their **order documentation** (and surveying process) seem simple – indeed, without exception they offered to complete the administration for me. I could **customize** (of course within limits) any one of each company's double glazing ranges to suit my house and my subjective preferences, and each variation was made as apparently **affordable** as I wanted by mixing the numbers according to **different payment systems** and by including 'special' offers and discounts. Each company belonged to at least one professional **trade association**, and I was given the choice of when I wanted the job started and when I wanted the **split** between replacing the upstairs and downstairs windows. Between them, the companies reflected near perfect competition, as far as their Sales and Product Elements (including price) were considered.

And yet, only one of the eight companies I spoke with went beyond these obvious and tangible Factors – at least in *my* perception – by also offering me satisfaction with two other elements important to me. These were the *cultural* and what I call the 'pre-sales' elements. Culturally, the quality of salesmanship was much more in keeping with the company's acknowledgement that I was making a capital purchase, than other companies which were keen to push their products with no regard for the time and space I needed to make a decision of that magnitude.

> Secondly, the quality of their pre-sales service exceeded my expectations, when the salesman offered to use his company's internal trade contacts to find replacement wall tiles for two out-of-production tiles I could not find in regular high street DIY stores. That company, T and K Double Glazing, a small privately-owned business, won the contract.

Satisfaction Element (3) After-sales

Factor	Excellence is:
Maintained interest	Acknowledging and honouring a customer's 'lifetime value' (see page 69) to the company and not disillusioning genuinely loyal customers by failing to acknowledge (and reward) that loyalty (see Chapter 7); ensuring that the reordering procedure is simple and builds on existing information about customers.
Complaint handling	Empowered staff responding immediately, courteously, honestly, sympathetically and thoroughly; keeping the customer advised throughout the complaint-management process; and using technology as a tool, not as an overlord.
	(Throughout the Sales and After-sales processes it is essential to attune the business to *customers'* contact requirements)

改

RICOH TECHNO NET

Ricoh Techno Net (RTN) was formed from Ricoh Service in 1988. It remains a wholly-owned subsidiary of the Ricoh Group, responsible for fulfilling the after-care objectives of the group's camera and office-equipment sales. RTN has been voted second-best After-care service company by the Japan Association of After-care Service Management for four consecutive years, since January 1991 when Mr Yamashita took over presidency of the company from Ricoh head-quarters.

Despite having worked for Ricoh for many years, Mr Yamashita recognized how little he knew about RTN, the After-care market, and a customer-care programme – the 'Better Presentation Movement' – that he discovered had been launched in RTN in 1988. This was still current, but had apparently failed to make any measurable impact. By April 1991 he had formulated 'Vision 93', a strategic customer-satis-faction plan designed to revive the Better Presentation Movement, remotivate RTN employees and create a new values framework based on RTN becoming a learning organization through building inti-mate (or learning) relationships with customers.

Yamashita's first (and most radical) action was to delegate his presidential responsibilities and spend a *year* in the field listening to RTN customer engineers and winning their hearts and minds to his vision of excellence in After-sales service. His central message was 'humanity' – turning After-sales service from a purely mechanistic process to one based firmly on relationships between internal and external customers. Second, he raised technical knowledge tenfold through a substantial education programme, and initiated a three-way strategic information exchange system between RTN, its engi-neers and its customers.

Finally, he initiated a programme of face-to-face discussions with customers, to go beyond the statistical data recorded on paper-based customer surveys. He concentrated not only on customers who were 'dissatisfied' but also on those who were 'fairly satisfied'. His view is that 'fairly' is not good enough and, in any case, 'fairly sat-isfied' customers are easy prey for competitors.

As Yamashita says about RTN's After-sales satisfaction pro-gramme: 'No compromise. No resignation. No excuses.'

Satisfaction Element (4) Location

Factor	Excellence is:
Location	Explaining the location precisely (in text, graphics or verbally) and ensuring that any changes to access roads (layout, names or numbers) or to public transport which serves the area are incorporated in current directions
Access	Clearly signposting the location, *ideally* on all access points within a five-mile radius; and ensuring that all the exterior faces of buildings, gateways and drives and all company land reflect the corporate image and convey an empathy with customers
Security and comfort	Providing adequate lighting, cover and signage to all car parks and entranceways; ensuring that the total internal environment conforms to all relevant health and safety regulations; and ensuring that the physical space serves the needs of the dynamics of human interaction
Provision for customers with special needs	Ensuring that nothing discriminates against special-needs groups

Whoever it was who replied 'Location, location, location!' to the question 'What is important in business?' got it right (well, partly right). The distributive trades know this well. Each major retailer has vied with every other for prime sites on high streets and in the new out-of-town shopping centres; and the location of distribution depots is critical to minimizing downstream costs and delivery time. Hotels also know how important location is to attracting particular target customers. But the Location Factors also include those which have an

改

impact on the customer micro-environment: **convenience of access, security and comfort** (factors high on the public agenda following the James Bulger kidnap case in the UK and other abduction and personal attack incidents), and provision for customers with special needs (a factor highlighted by the activities of disabled and equal-opportunity lobby and pressure groups for many years).

The Time Element, too, is important for any type of customer, but more so for retail customers at certain times and seasons and for international traders, for whom business is driven by a 24-hour clock.

Satisfaction Element (5) Time

Factor	Excellence is:
Business hours	Providing a service according to customers' needs, not according to the presence or absence of competitors
Applicability and availability of products	Providing a choice of continuously improved products that are relevant to current needs and purchase patterns
Speed of transactions	Ensuring the process is as *short* as customers want it

---

THE HIGH-STREET CLEARING BANKS

Martin Taylor, Barclays Bank Chief Executive has said, 'The idea has lodged in the popular mind that the banks are inconsiderate, brutal, greedy and incompetent.' Surely there has never been a truer admission of the popular perception of UK banks.

Yet even though this is universally recognized and customers have lost a great deal of confidence in the system, the clearing banks have been astonishingly slow to do anything about changing their image and rebuilding their relationships with customers.

Sir Brian Piman, Lloyds Chief Executive has said, 'Customers want convenience, efficiency, quick answers ...' – and to be treated as adults.

First Direct, Midland Bank's telephone banking subsidiary appears to have achieved the right balance between operating profitably and providing the quality of service that is attracting an increasing number of customers. First Direct's Managing Director, Kevin Newman, describes the service as 'personable rather than personal' and that the bank is endeavouring to offer 'an adult-to-adult relationship'.

Satisfaction Element (6) Culture

Factor	Excellence is:
Ethics*	Being unquestionably legal, non-discriminatory, moral and above board
Conduct	Being unprejudiced, willingly dutiful, objective, even-handed, honest, unimpeachable and authentically customer-focused; and learning from constructive criticism
Internal relationships	Demonstrating fair and equitable treatment of all employees, with no 'unjustifiable' disparities between the highest and lowest members of staff; understanding the concept of the *internal* customer (*see* Chapter 4); providing opportunities for self- and managed multi-skills development; trusting staff with information and decision-making power; encouraging involvement, team identity and contribution; favouring cross-functional collaboration; and ensuring *everyone* understands, accepts and acts out their personal customer-facing mission
External relationships	Developing a *partnership* with suppliers and customers, rather than acting as if discrete parties should be separated by the control exerted by a superior over a

改

	subordinate (Bearing in mind the unprecedented power in the hands of today's customers, it is worth noting that the 'superior' might, in fact, be the customer!)
Quality of purchase experience	Creating a feeling that is wholly consistent with customers' rights to receive total care and satisfaction, and by which each 'moment of service truth'* is an absolute confirmation of the primacy of customers in corporate culture, values and policy

See also the Co-operative Bank's ethical policy on page 126

The Culture Element is, perhaps, the most formative in motivating a company's offering for it determines – in terms of the corporate mission, values, ethics and standards – how the company will relate to its stakeholders and for what qualities it and its employees will be known.

A company's culture will be assessed by customers asking of it such questions as:

- does the company trade legally and ethically?
- can I trust the company and its people?
- does the company demonstrate financial probity and prudence?
- does the company treat *all* its employees equally, fairly and as people?
- is the company environmentally responsible?
- will I be treated as a real person or as an administrative 'cipher'?
- does it trade equitably with its suppliers?
- are its standards convergent with mine and society's?

---

* This phrase was coined by Jan Carlzon, president of Scandinavian Airline Systems.

There is probably little doubt that, irrespective of the quality of the deliverables in the other five elements, organizations like British Gas, British Airways, the UK's Conservative Government, Lonhro, General Motors, News Corporation, T and N – to list just a few recognized names – have each lost support in their time because ordinary supporters, customers and shareholders were disillusioned by some aspect of their Cultural conduct; and so fundamental is culture to perception that simply announcing the resignation of an executive, changing a product, retraining the sales force, or issuing a charter will not of themselves completely undo cultural mismanagement. Some of the major financial institutions, for example, have a lot of trust to rebuild following the way their personal financial representatives have misinformed thousands of customers; Benetton's culture, also, has been questioned as a consequence of its radical poster-advertising campaign. Customers ask, if the company's culture permits selling (or marketing) like this, what else does it find ethically acceptable?

None of the above lists of factors is entirely exhaustive, but they nonetheless underscore two key points:

1 Too many negative perceptions or experiences and a customer will believe they will not get the level of customer service and satisfaction they know is their right, and which might be given by an alternative supplier. Customer care is a positive discriminator.

2 No single Element or set of Factors by themselves will deliver complete customer satisfaction – because each of the six contributes something to the overall purchase decision. A brilliant Sales Element can be tarnished by a poor After-sales Element; a perfect Product Element can be wasted if the Location Element fails to satisfy; five of the Elements can be in place only to lose ground due to a negatively-perceived Culture Element.

TEXAS INSTRUMENTS

Even though Texas Instruments was known for its reliable products, innovatory software and an extensive network of professional dealers, the company was consistently ranked last among major minicomputer manufacturers during the 1980s due to its corporate culture. This was perceived to be so product- and cost-oriented, it overshadowed the effects of the other elements.

EASTERN AIRLINES

The corporate culture within Eastern Airlines was developed in the late 1980s from an emphasized focus on product and cost to include satisfaction of customers' needs, yet the change failed to deliver its intended benefits because the company's products (its routes and aircraft) did not meet passengers' needs, and potential customers were barely motivated by the airline's poor image in the marketplace.

It is that second point which goes some way towards explaining why customer charters – the Citizen's Charter, for example (see page 3) – often (but not always) fail to achieve their intent wholly: behind their publication is a customer-care vacuum, in which nothing or very little in terms of management processes, staff training and empowerment, quality, improvement and culture – throughout the organization – will have been developed to support in depth a charter's promises. It is these Factors, especially those within the Culture Element, that will project the initial concept and vision of customer care excellence.

Many charters are suspected of being a self-serving marketing exercise. And the same point helps explain why many – not all – customer-care initiatives which *only* look outward fail to impress: on the one hand, companies develop just the obvious and tangible Satisfaction Elements; on the other, they make customer service the responsibility of just one team (the Customer Services Department) where, even though staff are trained and are served by interactive software, this nevertheless functions like a customer charter – a veneer behind which (in other departments, in other functions) the old attitudes, behaviours, processes and values continue largely undeveloped and unchanged.

Thus, part of the answer to the question posed in the title of this Chapter, what makes excellent customer care? is, *all six Satisfaction Elements must be developed and delivered concurrently to achieve the quality and depth of care promoted in this book.*

Excellence

The second part of the answer comes from considering the 'What' in the title question; in other words, what attitudes and behaviour make the customer care offered truly excellent rather than merely mundane? The answer to this question is presented in the right-hand column of the previous table, which listed broad standards of excellence against a number of each Satisfaction Element Factors. Clearly, however, different companies and different industries will have different expressions of these standards, which are more suited to their markets and the customers served.

K.K. AUTO WAVES

K.K. Auto Waves is in direct competition with 20 other motor parts retailers in its immediate neighbourhood. Despite the fact that the shop is in a secondary location away from the main traffic flow, sales have increased tenfold in three years.

Customers are willing to travel to the store because of its reputation for high-quality service and low prices unobtainable anywhere else.

Hitoshi Hirooka has been steeped in the car parts business for nearly 40 years. He turned away safe job offers when he was a young man to try his luck with a small company then called Taiho Industry K.K., but which became Auto Backs Seven, the biggest car parts supplier in Japan. He helped Auto Backs grow to its current pre-eminent position and then quit to start a wholesale engine oil business, K.K.Auto Waves.

The key to K.K.Auto Waves's success is Hirooka's management philosophy. He believes that operations manuals and systems are completely irrelevant. He believes that if you educate your staff to satisfy customers rather than make sales, those customers will keep coming back.

▶

▶

He leaves it to his staff to work out stock and pricing policies and concentrates on customer-care approaches. Hirooka sees himself more as an educator, introducing necessary disciplines to make the soil more fertile. He is fond of agricultural metaphors: 'In agriculture, turning and cleansing the soil gives birth to fruit. You only need good quality seed and fertiliser once you have carefuly tilled the earth.'

He also has a clear idea about the efficacy of discipline – it must be clear, specific, simple and easy to put into practice.

When rival operators visit K.K. Auto Waves to seek out the key to its success, Hirooka, now President and Chairman, always advises them to go back to their own shops, study their own employees and customers, and thus find the source of their problems.

He doesn't believe in amassing data because, 'You cannot find specific and efficient solutions until you separate each problem into very small units. You simply end up allowing your staff to duck their responsibilities if you let them hide behind written reports.' Auto Waves eschews regular staff meetings, but leaves it to individual staff to carry through the philosophy of concentrating on customers.

Hirooka believes forms, manuals and systems throttle originality and creativity and the opportunities for personal growth. New problems invariably arise but the speed and flexibility with which they are dealt depend on the common sense, ability and enthusiasm of the staff themselves.

Hirooka is prepared to accept losses on some items because that way he doesn't lose customers. If a customer is satisfied because, for example, he has found some obscure part for an uncommon make of vehicle – even if it is sold at a loss – he will also make other more profitable purchases later.

Servicing foreign cars and installing parts bought elsewhere are intrinsically unprofitable but again they lead to highly-satisfied customers who may well buy more expensive items.

Hirooka propounds a subtle philosophy for business development: 'If you can fulfill one previously unserved need of one out of a thousand customers, you may have found a need of one thousand people that you haven't served before. A good retail business is one where a need is noticed.'

Of course, these standards of excellence are not wholly universal: industrial and retail customers have different expectations; however, they are not so different that the above list cannot serve as a model of high-level care irrespective of your market sector. The goal is to identify the key drivers of *your* customers' satisfaction expectations.

Geoffrey Colvin, assistant managing editor of *Fortune* magazine, has written: 'The consumer is definitely in the *mood* to be demanding .... As a result, brand loyalty is eroding and consumers are increasingly telling researchers that they will not go back to spending [in] the way they used to.' He asks the question, 'In a world of falling margins, nearly perfect information, increasingly perfect competition, and demanding buyers, how will smart companies compete?' His answer is far from complete, but it reflects much of what I have said so far in this book: 'I strongly believe it will be through human interaction (which must have the right foundation culture) and highly-personal customer service – which reaches deep into the buyer's psyche... and which all people will increasingly hunger for.' He goes on to say, 'The opportunity to understand the new consumer ... is probably one of the richest you will ever meet.'[4]

LIFETIME VALUE

'Lifetime value' is not a new concept. It is one that was first used by direct marketing (particularly mail order) organizations in the United States from about 1956, but like so many 'hidden gems' it took a long time to surface and be valued by industrial and other retail organizations (such as banks, supermarkets and hotels) as a reasonably accurate measure of a customer's worth.

Calculating lifetime value is straightforward:

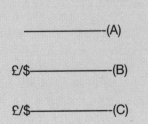

1 Note the number of customers served in the present year. ——————————(A)

2 Identify the gross costs of gaining and maintaining their custom. £/$————————(B)

3 Identify the profit generated from sales to them. £/$————————(C)

---

4 G. Colvin, Assistant Managing Editor, *Fortune* magazine, writing in '*Customer Care, A Director's Guide*', Institute of Directors and Unisys Ltd, 1994

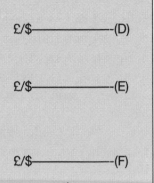

4 Subtract (B) from (C) to give the net
   contribution.   £/$————————(D)

5 Divide (D) by the number of customers in
   (A) to give an average individual net
   present value.   £/$————————(E)

6 Multiply (E) by the number of years you
   can expect to retain each individual's
   custom, to give their potential lifetime
   value (at today's £ or $ value).   £/$————————(F)

Clearly, the more that is known about your customers the more precise and useful will be the figures which, in turn, will also answer the
more profound question, *What could it cost the company if we fail to
provide customer satisfaction?*

Thus, the complete answer to the question, what makes excellent customer care? is:

1 Each of the six Satisfaction Elements must be concurrently developed and delivered.

2 An organizational culture must exist that is sustained internally by
   people-centred management processes, is stimulated externally by
   known customers' needs, and which delivers satisfaction (and
   reward) in excess of customers' expectations.

MARRIOTT LODGING INTERNATIONAL[5]

Marriott International Inc. was created in October 1993, when Marriott Corporation split into two separate companies. Marriott International comprises the lodging and service businesses. It has
operations in 50 American states and 24 countries. The company has
approximately 200,000 employees, who make up to 20 million customer contacts each day.

---

5 E. Fuller, Executive Vice President and Managing Director Marriott Lodging
  International, writing in '*Customer Care, A Director's Guide*', Institute of Directors and Unisys Ltd, 1994

The company's philosophy, first engendered by its founder J.W. Marriott senior, is that success is never final but is always an ongoing process of growth and change and that, if Marriott treats its employees well, they will look after customers.

This approach served the company very well, but it recognized that even this would not be sufficient to ensure continuing success into the next century, so Marriott's own brand of total quality management was born. It faced a major change in its culture from a procedural to a 'whatever it takes' approach to servicing customer needs.

Key Lessons

There are a number of lessons which Marriott learnt during the development of its quality programme.

Key among these was that commitment to the whole quality-management process had to come from the top. Marriott asked a lot of its staff in developing the empowerment concept – their time, trust and commitment. Only when it was clear that the most senior management were also committed to the idea did the process begin to take shape.

Another lesson, for Marriott and other companies considering a similar approach, is that there are no 'off the peg' customer-care solutions. Companies must work within their own culture, and to the capabilities of management and staff.

Customer care is not a 'quick fix' solution to a company's problems. It must be developed gradually: customer-focused companies evolve, they don't appear overnight.

Customer needs and preferences are constantly evolving, so ongoing research and testing to ensure a constant dialogue with customers is also essential.

Finally, the process should not be allowed to take command of the results: companies should never lose sight of the fundamental objectives of customer care.

The Move Towards Customer Focus

During the late 1980s, a combination of increased competition in the global hotel market, an oversupply of hotel rooms in the US and tougher economic conditions led Marriott to look at how it could improve its market position.

▶

改

The company recognized that success would not come solely from changing the product or offering cheaper prices, but from having better, more customer-focused and responsive staff than its competitors; so in 1987 Marriott began working on its total-quality programme.

Many companies were developing quality-management programmes at this time, but some appeared to be concentrating on gaining quality awards at the expense of their own business objectives, and Marriott did not wish to fall into this trap.

Benchmarking

During 1990 Marriott's most senior managers visited some of the company's suppliers, including Milliken, AT & T and Fed-Ex, all of which are widely recognized for their customer responsiveness, and looked at how their quality programmes worked.

Customer Perceptions

Marriott also looked carefully at factors which influenced customer perceptions of service in its hotels.

One such factor is that guests deal primarily with doormen, housekeepers, food and beverage servers, so the customer's view of a hotel and of the company as a whole is generally formed by the behaviour of front-line staff.

It followed that service quality could be enhanced by giving greater responsibility to staff who have customer contact; so empowerment became one of the key elements in Marriott's programme.

Empowerment

Empowerment gives all Marriott staff – known as associates – the responsibility to act for the benefit of the customer. It allows staff to take action, within prescribed limits, to avert or solve problems without first having to gain approval from their manager or superior. In this way, most customer problems and complaints can be prevented, rather than put right once they have occurred. Where problems do arise, empowered staff can solve them without delay and, where appropriate, make amends.

A situation which could cause a guest to leave their hotel with a bad impression of Marriott can be turned into a positive one, and enhance customer loyalty, if properly handled. It requires associates to understand the principles behind empowerment and to use judgement in deciding what action to take.

Implementation
New management procedures, staff training, and a fundamental culture change were crucial, as was a sensitive approach to handling mistakes. Staff who misjudged situations, or who were overzealous in making amends for minor problems, had to be coached without discouraging them from taking the initiative again. The process concentrated on three areas:

- creating enthusiasm among the staff to achieve clearly defined goals
- developing skills to enable employees to solve problems
- developing company culture to accommodate continuous improvement rather than static performance targets.

Trust and Confidence
Empowerment requires trust and confidence from managers and their staff. The system assures associates that their ideas will be listened to, and that actions will have the support of management.

Involving staff in the decision-making process enhances their sense of worth within the organization, and can pay dividends in terms of reduced costs and service improvements: the staff who do the actual work often know better than their managers how procedures work 'on the ground' and can identify ways of streamlining them.

London Marriott Initiative
A recent example of this was the London Marriott hotel in Grosvenor Square. The problem involved the speedy removal of room-service trays from bedroom corridors. Room-service attendants were responsible for clearing trays, but it was difficult to keep the corridors clear at all times. A team of associates worked on the problem, researching the situation, and developing solutions.

The result was a change of responsibility so that all staff who see trays in corridors remove them. To encourage staff to participate, each tray carries a sticker which is saved by the person retrieving the tray. These can then be exchanged for a range of gifts, such as a bottle of wine or dinner in the restaurant.

▶

Not only did this speed up removal of trays, it also reduced the time room attendants spent looking for trays, freeing them for other tasks.

Cross Training

Another element of the quality programme was cross training of associates. By training staff to perform several job functions within the hotel, Marriott has found that staff are motivated by greater variety and, in some cases, more responsibility in their jobs. The hotel benefits from having a more flexible and better-trained workforce.

Trickle Down Versus Bottom Up

An undertaking as large and diverse as Marriott's quality initiative inevitably had to overcome a number of obstacles, such as initial scepticism among staff. This was particularly evident where staff wanted to maintain procedures they were used to and were concerned about the disruption to established work practices.

Marriott first approached the change from the bottom up, believing that if the most junior staff were able to work in a different way this would give the more senior staff confidence in the programme.

It became clear that 'trickle down' from the most senior management was also required, because staff had to see and believe that senior management were totally committed.

There was some initial resentment of the time required to implement the new initiatives. Some staff saw time spent in problem-solving, meetings and training as a conflict with their existing work. This largely disappeared as the process progressed.

Impact on Management

Though conflicts were anticipated, there were pitfalls which had not been planned for: it was necessary, for example, to convince staff that it was not just 'this year's staff-motivation programme' but an ongoing process of change.

Marriott's empowerment process has resulted in a more energized, creative and forthcoming workforce. Ideas are flowing from staff in all functions and at all levels. It has also had an impact on managers' roles, making them more people-oriented: empowerment does not fit with a dictatorial management style.

Results

Marriott has learnt a great deal about its staff and managers during the quality process.

One is that staff – including hourly-paid manual staff – can be trusted to use their judgement in dealing with problems.

Further Development

There remains work to be done in some areas, for instance in maintaining consistency across all Marriott hotels. This is central to the Marriott brand. The same in-room amenities must be available in San Francisco, Warsaw and Hong Kong, and this is important to business travellers.

Some hotels have introduced more service enhancements than others so the challenge is to control initiatives at the most active hotels without dampening enthusiasm, and help properties which are further behind to catch up. Quality is an ongoing process at Marriott with continuous staff training and development at hotels around the world.

I can personally vouch for the quality and success of Marriott's customer-care programme and its staff training, when I stayed at their hotel in Leeds, having booked facilities for a management workshop, I was met by the Banqueting Manager who gave clear, concise guidelines for both equipment and domestic arrangements for the day. In most hotels that I have used for running programmes this is standard behaviour, but it is usually from this point on that I have found myself operating in a void, with little care and attention from the Banqueting Manager (a telephone extension as a helpline is usually the limit). This was not the case with the manager in Leeds. I not only had his telephone extension, but he made a point of checking out our group in person throughout the day to ensure everything was running smoothly. His involvement extended to being aware of the theme of our course, and when I suddenly realized that I had forgotten to book a syndicate room, he told me that he would 'empower himself', and offer me an adjoining room free of charge (as we only needed it for a brief session). This offer, he continued, could only last for the first day, and if I required a syndicate room for day two I would need to book a room and there would be a charge. He noticed, however, that

改

ideally we needed more than one room as space was somewhat limited, and even though it was inconvenient to him, as he was already overseeing a large group who were taking coffee in the reception, he suggested we used a specific area within reception which did not inconvenience the other party. On the following day when he came to clear the room after our session had finished, I told him how pleased we all were by the way he had taken care of us. He seemed genuinely pleased by the compliment, and in his own words 'positive feedback was always gratefully received!' He and his staff proved Marriott's customer-orientation: he was a reliable source, confident and well-trained, actively seeking an opportunity to exceed my expectations. The question I asked myself after I had left was, why should I go anywhere else in the future?

Another case worth presenting for a company's responsiveness to its customers concerns Oranda-Ya (literally Holland House) Bakery and Confectioners in Chiba City, Japan:

ORANDA-YA BAKERY AND CONFECTIONERS

The Oranda-Ya business was established just after the war by Hiroshi Ikeda and his father, after the latter returned wounded from the war. In order to feed his family, Ikeda's father baked *Koppe-pan* (a Japanese bread) in his back garden, using his weekly flour ration.

At the age of seventeen, Hiroshi started baking to order for other families but didn't really possess the necessary skills, so he managed to find a bakery to teach him the craft within just one month.

His early efforts failed, but his determination paid off and soon his bakery became celebrated for its Koppe-pan and also for a number of Western-style confectionery lines.

Hiroshi joined forces with his brother, Takao, to sell his own brand of confectionery called *Oranda-ya*. The business took off rapidly and within ten years the two brothers had built up a chain of shops.

Whenever a new item is introduced, each shop is supplied with a photograph of the product and data about the ingredients. Each shop decides its own product-range mix and stocking policy, depending on the locality and customer profile; each also handles its own sales promotion. As many purchases are gifts for special occasions, customers are often particularly demanding about the content of each item they buy, so sales staff need extensive product knowledge.

A regular 'Product Meeting' is held between the company's directors and the marketing staff during which they sift through the customer research which is carried out at each shop. This research throws up requests for product changes and also stimulates ideas from sales staff – for example, the need for a specialized gift-wrapping service.

The key to Oranda-ya's success has always been a carefully-balanced blend of high-quality production, innovative sales techniques and ongoing development.

Even if a customer likes a particular product, he or she soon tires of it, so it is necessary to vary recipes carefully from time to time. In order to achieve this, the firm is constantly seeking ideas and opinions from their customers. For example, their 'Tulip Doll' sweet, an improved version of 'Tulip Sablee,' is a result of customer comments that the previous version was too large and there was insufficient variety in each box.

Customers also expressed a preference for the sweets to be packed in boxes rather than tins because it was more environmentally friendly.

This close interaction between the company and its customers helps to retain the image of Oranda-ya as a specialist baker and confectioner.

Oranda-ya has two factories producing Japanese and Western products. The fully-automated cake factory produces 40 varieties of a ten-cake product range. The production process is carefully recorded on 'Operation Order Sheets' and a quick-delivery system of perishable ingredients is operated to ensure absolute freshness. The firm also now sells *Fuwadora*, a steamed bun filled with bean-jam and cream which has only a one-day shelf life.

Because of changing seasonal demand, there is a direct ordering system between the factories and individual shops. A highly-sophisticated computerized ordering and production system calculates on a daily basis productivity per employee, personnel costs, gross margins, raw material requirements, etc.

A 'Rape Blossoms Card' has been introduced – a customer loyalty scheme offering gifts and vouchers, depending on the level of purchases. The 75,000 customers who have already joined the scheme also receive a variety of direct-mail literature as well as being asked to participate in taste trials.

改

Summary

- The essence of the Kaizen approach to customer care is to take the idea and practice of customer service deep into a company, and once there continuously to improve its quality.

- The six Satisfaction Elements are:

  1 The Product Element.

  2 The Sales Element.

  3 The After-sales Element.

  4 The Location Element.

  5 The Time Element.

  6 The Culture Element.

- All six elements must be developed and delivered concurrently to provide truly excellent customer care.

- 'Lifetime value' is a reasonably accurate forecast of the worth of each existing customer to a company. That value is also a measure of what it will cost the company if, because it fails to offer excellent customer care, the customer becomes an ex-customer.

- The foundation of excellent customer care is not only built from the six Satisfaction Elements but also from internal processes that are people-centred, sound market research and an adequate and sustainable budget.

PART II

ASPECTS
OF THE
KAIZEN
APPROACH
TO
CUSTOMER
CARE

5

BREAKING
DOWN
INTERNAL
BARRIERS

改

INTRODUCTION

T
here is a marked difference between a Kaizen company and a non-Kaizen one in the style of interaction that exists between employees. It is easy to imagine (or remember) how in the latter, employees, who were once treated indifferently – as 'units of labour' – were compelled to relate in an involuntary or deterministic way with little conscious thought about the cause and effect of their unassenting relationships with fellow employees. In this type of environment there was a poverty of discretional behaviour and plain common courtesy and politeness. Now, this might be an extreme picture of what once was, but it serves as a contrast to the consenting and dedicated behaviour in a Kaizen company where internal relationships are resolutely fostered as the oil which lubricates collaboration. In *this* environment fellow employees are treated as internal customers deserving the same consciously courteous, attentive and sensitive attitudes as external customers. (*See also* The Rights and Responsibilities of Colleagues, later in this Chapter.)

SENIOR MANAGEMENT'S RESPONSIBILITY

Many companies, especially American ones (for example, Marriott International and Mars), have taken a step towards overcoming the mental block that often precludes a perception of colleagues as customers, by describing staff as *associates*. This is hardly a revolutionary step (more evolutionary), but the word 'associate' has a connotated image of a person being a *part* of a company (which 'employees' are) and yet at the same time set apart. This separateness lends a feeling that peers and colleagues should be accorded the same respect that customers (also separate from the company) are shown. In this prevailing atmosphere senior management will find it easier motivating staff to:

- be approachable, available and attentive (to everyone, but especially to their own direct internal customers)
- flag relationship problems before they become compromisingly dysfunctional
- understand that internal relationship or task problems can affect the quality of external relationships
- treat others as individuals who, if not actually, are potentially their equal
- share information and resources
- communicate with each other using means, and at those times, most appropriate to others' preferences and needs
- provide constructive feedback
- develop professional and active relationships (rather than passive, reactive or accidental references to others)
- accept the concept of co-workers as internal customers whose contribution should be neither taken for granted (simply because they also are employees) nor undervalued nor unthanked
- understand that a culture based on *internal* customers will echo and reinforce a drive to satisfy *external* customers.

Senior managers (including members of a top team) should each dedicate between 40 to 45 per cent of their time, during the early phases of a customer-care initiative, to coaching and counselling for improved internal relationships and attitudes. Their involvement at this magnitude will help mitigate the cynicism that can grow among staff, who hear senior management paying lip service to the initiative but never see them change their own behaviour to be consistent with the new strategy.

ZX

WHO ARE MY INTERNAL CUSTOMERS?

The question, Who are my internal customers? has yet to be answered. It is too trite to reply 'Every other member of the company', though in a Kaizen company where cross-functionalism, team-based working, enablement and all-points responsibility for external-customer care is *de riguer*, it *is* reasonable to say this. However, day-to-day reality in a pre-Kaizen Western company is more pragmatic, and a truer answer will be revealed for each person in a personal communications map.

COMMUNICATION MAPPING

A communications map is similar to a spider diagram: it depicts the connections between related objects, in this case the connections between individuals in a company; but a communications map is *not* an organogram, rather it depicts who relates to whom – in other words, a person's internal customers – along *task-related* channels of communication.

To draw a map is relatively simple. Ideally, however, it should be as comprehensive as possible. The diagram on page 80 is an illustration of how this might look.

You will also need to indicate any links – the 'cross links' between the people you have shown- which do/could have a direct bearing on the fulfilment of your tasks. For example, Richard in Marketing will usually refer to Oliver in Sales before responding to your monthly communication; similarly, John, Adrian and Maurice might have to confer before you receive the information/resource you need, and Brian appears to do nothing without first deferring to Diane.

Once your map is in place you will need to indicate by some form of coding, say broken, or zigzag lines, the regularity of contact – be it, daily, once a week, once a month or only spasmodically. Also, ideally, the means by which you mainly interact with that person (eg P = personal (face to face), E = E-mail, T = telephone, etc.). Some lines will obviously carry more than one code letter.

This illustration will indicate to you your internal customers – in other words, those on whom you depend for the quality, quantity,

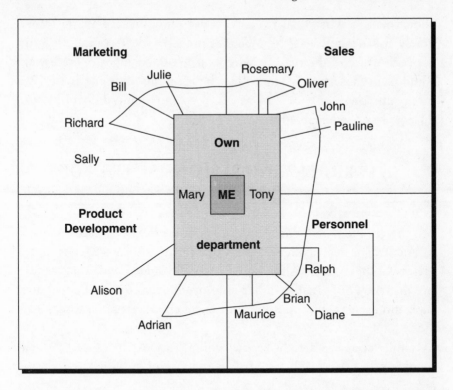

cost and time of your work. They similarly depend on you, for the lines you have drawn represent *two-way* channels of communication.

The fundamental purpose of drawing a communications map is to highlight where communication needs to be improved, so the next step in the process would be with a red biro to indicate where communication channels are poor and with a green one where they are good.

In this manner you can actually isolate individuals or departments, plus the current mode of communication devices you use with them, so you can start moving forward with correcting the situation. Before beginning, it can be very revealing to make a list of the ultimate repercussions that a weak link in communication can have (this will usually end up with poor service to the external customer, as without internal harmony and clarity between people, processes and departments, the needs of external customers can never be fully addressed).

Some of the reasons why your red communication channels can fail could range from, for example, 'He/she dislikes receiving memos' or, 'He never bothers to answer his telephone' to, 'I don't know enough

改

about his/her work/task needs to be communicated in the most timely/appropriate way' or, '(Name) prevents clear communication between us'; and the reasons why your green channels operate well could be because, for instance, 'He/she is on my wavelength' or, 'We can count on each other to respond to our communications' or, 'He/she has been enabled to act.'

THE RIGHTS AND RESPONSIBILITIES OF COLLEAGUES

An environment in which colleagues and co-workers are seen as internal customers challenges everyone to strive for excellence in the quality of their relationships and, hence, the quality and effectiveness of what they do. Treating other employees as customers contributes substantially to the achievement of excellent external customer service.

Employees have a right to the willing support of others in their company, but these rights are balanced by responsibilities:

Rights

Internal customers have a right to expect and receive:

- courtesy and respect
- information germane to their tasks
- resources necessary for the completion of their tasks
- freedom and opportunity to express views and opinions which contribute to decisions affecting their work
- understanding, if a request of them is unreasonable or prejudicial to their personal beliefs or needs
- support to fulfil corporate and/or department objectives
- honest, ethical, moral and legal conduct from colleagues and superiors.

These rights derive not only from basic human concerns but also from an individual's role in the service chain.

Responsibilities

These are the other side of the same coin, and therefore include:

- being available, approachable and responsive
- listening fairly and uncritically to others' views and opinions
- sharing decision-making when this affects others' work
- providing requested information and resources
- being aware of others' personal beliefs and needs and taking account of them when making requests
- honouring these responsibilities by being consciously aware of other people.

Respecting another person's rights and meeting one's own responsibilities stems obviously from an attitude of mind and, however hackneyed it sounds, it remains true that every service chain is wholly dependent on the interactions between internal people without whose co-operation and collective dedication to service the ultimate people, *external* customers, will be poorly served. As Steve Norman, Regional General Manager of Canon (UK) has said, 'You cannot even start to examine the issue of pleasing customers until you have satisfied and happy employees.'

Summary

- Senior management has the responsibility for ensuring that the prevailing culture encourages internal-customer relationships; team leaders have the responsibility for ensuring employees are trained and motivated to respect relationship rights and responsibilities.

- A communications map will help identify each person's direct internal customers and the communication channels which link them and serve the service chain.

- While procedures and systems exist to streamline workflow and resource efficiency, the service chain is dependent on people whose collaboration is essential to the effective provision of external customer satisfaction.

改

NB. *The need for employers to care for the emotional health of their employees is becoming increasingly established in law in the UK, as claims of discrimination (and bullying) are filed at court and in industrial tribunals against companies and individuals. It is not inconceivable that 'emotional health' will come to include internal relationships per se and the provisions which a company makes for the training and development of its staff (see next Chapter).*

6

MOTIVATING
AND
ENABLING
EMPLOYEES

改

INTRODUCTION

Providing excellent customer care is not a clever game in improving employees' manners, though this can be all that separates a customer from a sale:

THE EX-CUSTOMER[6]

'I am a nice person. I'm the person who never complains, no matter what type of service I get.

'I'll go into a restaurant and stand and wait while the waiting staff gossip amongst themselves. I don't throw my weight around. If I get a bored or rude waiter I'll remain as polite as can be: I don't believe rudeness in return is the answer. I never nag and I never criticise, and I won't make a scene. I am a nice person; I am also the customer who never comes back.

'This is my way of reacting to poor service. That's why I take whatever is handed out, because I know I'll more than get even by not returning ... and by telling everyone I know not to bother buying from your business. This doesn't always relieve my frustrations, but it is far more deadly than blowing my top in front of other customers.

'There are a lot of nice customers like me. When we get pushed too far, we go somewhere else and spend our money where they are smart enough to employ people who appreciate customers.

'I laugh when I see you frantically spending your money on expensive advertising to get me back, when you could have had me for life

---

6 Author unknown

in the first place for a few kind words, a smile and a sincere "Thank you" for my patronage.

'It really doesn't matter what business you are in. Perhaps I've never heard of you or maybe you've never heard of me, but if you're finding business is bad perhaps there are too many people like me who actually have heard of you.'

HIGH-STREET RETAILERS IN THE UK

In January 1995, market research group, Grass Roots, published a report on the results of their customer service survey of 2500 high-street retailers in the UK. It appears to suggest that as a nation our reputation for surly service is still justified.

McDonald's, W.H.Smith and the John Lewis chain were among the well-known names criticized for making customers feel less than welcome. At W.H. Smith and John Menzies, staff were rated below average on knowledge, helpfulness, friendliness and eye contact. Barely half of them smiled, the report states. At other stores, customers had a problem getting staff to even acknowledge their presence.

Supermarkets, especially, fared poorly in terms of the customer friendliness displayed by their checkout staff. However, staff at gas and electricity showrooms, banks, post offices and railway stations rated highly in the survey: they were friendly, willing to explain and they inspired confidence.

Although the quality of service overall is better than it was ten years ago – according to the report – David Evans, chairman of Grass Roots, said, 'There is no room for complacency. Good service comes only from well-managed, well-motivated and well-trained staff.'

改

The Kaizen approach to customer care demands participation at a much deeper personal level than just a smile* and a cheerful 'thank you'; it depends on the *enablement* of employees. To put it simply, total employee performance in customer care depends on team leaders and senior management satisfying the improvement needs implicit in what I call the four-part enablement equation.

THE ENABLEMENT EQUATION

Employees – especially those in positions furthest from front line or direct customer-facing positions – will generally not 'Think Customer' intuitively. A development process will invariably be needed to help transform behaviours. The enablement equation is the heart of such a process. It can be explained as shown in the diagram below.

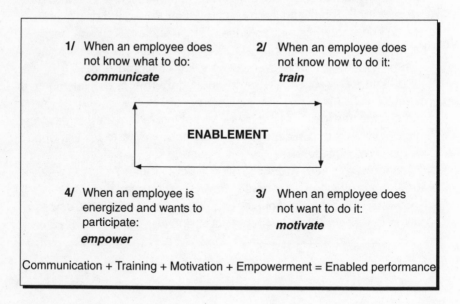

1/ When an employee does not know what to do: **communicate**

2/ When an employee does not know how to do it: **train**

ENABLEMENT

4/ When an employee is energized and wants to participate: **empower**

3/ When an employee does not want to do it: **motivate**

Communication + Training + Motivation + Empowerment = Enabled performance

---

* Dr. Karl Albrecht has referred to 'smile training' as like going through nothing more than a 'psychological car wash'.

善

Together, these four parts of the equation will produce employees who will think, decide and act proactively and intelligently according to their own perception of the good of customers and, hence, their company. However, the success of an employee-enablement programme will depend on the two further factors outside the immediate boundaries of the equation:

1 The Corporate Mission.

2 Employees' attitudes before programme introduction.

These, and the four parts of the enablement equation, are discussed below.

Corporate Mission

A shift to a Kaizen-based culture of customer service – indeed, a decision to become customer-focused per se – should be encapsulated in and driven by a formal mission statement, to which every activity in the company is geared and from which every employee gains his or her operational focus. Naturally, such an overarchingly important text must be worded precisely, communicated universally and frequently, and observed scrupulously by the CEO and his or her top team, especially. The statement must describe succinctly and unambiguously both the company's principal aims and its consequent internal culture and values. These must become the contextual framework onto which the activities in an employee-enablement programme must be designed to add the flesh.

Customer service is far too important a route to commercial success today for it to be perceived by either employees or external stakeholders (customers, suppliers, shareholders) as game playing. As Julian Richer, owner and Chairman of the 20-store chain of Richer Sounds hi-fi shops, has said, 'Old fashioned service is, paradoxically, the thing of the future. Tomorrow's businesses will learn that customers are not just people you sell cardboard boxes to on a one-off basis. If you want loyalty you have to look after your customers. And to do that you have to look after your staff, because they are not going to give great service unless they want to.' Richer sells his retailing experience to other firms, but more than that, he *'walks the talk'* – he exemplifies his company's mission to serve customers better than his competitors. And his staff see him, and his top team, as models worth emulating.

Employees' Attitudes

When Nissan took the decision to establish its UK car production plant in Sunderland, an unemployment blackspot, the company had the luxury of starting with the pick of staff from an almost limitless choice of potential employees (some of whom had applied from other regions in the UK), most of whom were already skilled or semi-skilled and used to an assembly line or engineering/technical culture. Nevertheless, Nissan was importing not only new job opportunities but also a new way of working – the Kaizen way.

As Nissan was entirely confident that its own craft-training pro-grammes would produce employees skilled to the company's stan-dards, a potential recruit's previous technical training and experience was less of an attractor than would have been the case had the appli-cant applied to a traditional manufacturing plant.

Given that Kaizen is a process-oriented business philosophy, Nissan identified (through assessment centres) recruits who demon-strated key personal and interpersonal process qualities. The qualities included open-mindedness, conceptualizing and learning ability, team orientation, flexibility and adaptability, self-discipline, an abil-ity to communicate ideas, loyalty, and respect for leadership. Atti-tude, innate motivation, information framework (that is, mindset) and perceptual attention were far more important than previous work history or age.

Onto this 'raw' material Nissan expertly grafted the Kaizen way of working (adapted to suit the national and local culture).

Not every company has Nissan's greenfield opportunity. As John Neill found when he decided to introduce Kaizen into Unipart, once a highly-unionised and wholly-owned part of British Leyland, it took an enormous effort by him and his top team to persuade his mature, established and initially sceptical workforce that Kaizen would work and, indeed, was necessary to ensure Unipart's survival as a privatized company.

That was just the first step. The next was to *deconstruct* the outmoded attitudes, styles of relationship, ways of working and internal processes before the new Kaizen culture, representing a paradigm shift from the old, could be introduced. A few employees did not make the transition successfully, and there were many small and large problems. It was an extraordinarily challenging time, but eventually the new corporate mission, values and processes replaced the rigid and constraining practices of the past. The development of the Kaizen environment continues, most notably in the creation of a knowledge-based culture.

The revival of Britain's motor industry workforces is one of the industrial success stories of the 1990s. Today, they are conscious that only customer satisfaction can provide real job security. As they are becoming more trusted to be enabled by a more enlightened management, they are becoming as culturally different from Red Robbo at British Leyland, as Red Robbo was from Mr Taiichi Ohno at Toyota.

OHASHI MANUFACTURING

Ohashi Manufacturing, headed by the company president Mr Ohashi, is a small manufacturer of mechatronic manpower saving devices.

It is a pioneer among small Japanese companies in that it recognized from as early as 1970 that employee participation in the business is vitally important. Ohashi's view is that for employees to feel motivated, and to maintain their motivation, they need opportunities to participate in management. Participation is in itself a form of training: it helps change employees' attitudes, develop more constructive suggestions and create an intelligent workforce.

There are at least six defined ways by which participation is encouraged:

- **The annual company strategy meeting.** All employees participate in a two-day meeting, during which company strategy is discussed and formulated. Eight different discussion groups are organized, covering every aspect of business planning. Drafts of a proposed strategy are available for two months before the meeting to allow everyone time to prepare their thoughts.

改

▶

- **The annual performance evaluation**. During this, each department's current performance is compared with the previous year. Concrete ideas for improvement are discussed. The main purpose is to identify areas where employees can improve departmental processes and performance during the year ahead.

- **Active involvement in designing improvements for each person's own area of work**. Visiting the Ohashi factory it is neither immediately impressive nor different from many other factories. Looking in detail at the areas where each person works, however, it becomes apparent how each employee has sought to improve their personal performance or working environment. For example, a standard issue tool box has been equipped with wheels to help its mobility; a mirror has been added to a piece of equipment to promote safety; the location of buttons on machines has been changed for convenience and added efficiency.

- **The open and warm atmosphere**. There are no barriers to communication either between departments or because of rank, power or age. At the **Innovative Management Training Meetings** held several times a year, for example, each department points out, in a constructive way, perceived problems and defects in other departments.

- *Ohashi Topics*. This is an occasional publication in which all employees can write exactly what they want. Contents include anything from detailed daily matters to company strategy.

- **Regarding everyone as a 'key person'**. A recent year's slogan was 'Each employee is a key person', ie each employee should be able to solve problems, have opinions and contribute fully to the organization.

THE ENABLEMENT EQUATION
Part 1 – Communicating

Communicating begins in a Kaizen company during the attitude-forming induction phase of a worker's employment, when he or she is first introduced to their company's mission, culture, strategies, processes, products, people and the team-support system. Induction can last up to a year in a Kaizen company in Japan, during which time the same factors will be communicated and experienced over and over again until the culture and way of working is learnt and becomes second nature.

Communicating in a Kaizen company has eight definite purposes. These are to:

1 Inform (that is, provide a framework of and for information).

2 Reinforce understanding (of 'how we do things here').

3 Engender openness.

4 Promote involvement (which 'is incompatible with closed and secretive organizations').

5 Motivate.

6 Enable.

7 Reinforce personal identity with a workteam, the company and its mission.

8 Maintain focus on customer satisfaction.

Clearly, communicating vertically and horizontally within a Kaizen organization is a critically important process in the team-based life of the company, and it is therefore a skill in which everyone is trained. This enables employees to contribute constructively and intelligently in team meetings, Quality Circles, Kaizen groups and their company's suggestion system. It will be remembered that because a team leader's interpersonal skills are continuously assessed by not only his or her managers but also his or her team, to ensure that as a prime communications conduit he or she remains capable of delivering and managing information, competence in making presentations, listening, discussion, counselling, giving feedback, brainstorming, report writing and interrogative techniques are core skills.

When first entering a Japanese production plant a visitor will be struck not just by the cleanliness and orderliness but also by the many progress, motivational and information signs, posters and charts hanging from the ceiling and pinned to vertical surfaces. These are important and an effective means of mass communication but, whereas Black and Decker installed high-tech electronics to communicate plant-wide at their County Durham factory, posters and charts are less expensive and much simpler though no less effective; indeed, to a Westerner's eyes there is a certain incongruity between hand-painted signs and the industriousness beneath them. But in Kaizen, simple is best – as Parker Knoll discovered (see page 46).

Kaizen organizations are keenly aware of the importance and value of communicating outside the company, especially to customers and suppliers. In Kaizen, the three-way partnership between a company, its first-tier suppliers and its customers is held together by a constant dialogue. (*See also* Chapter 7).

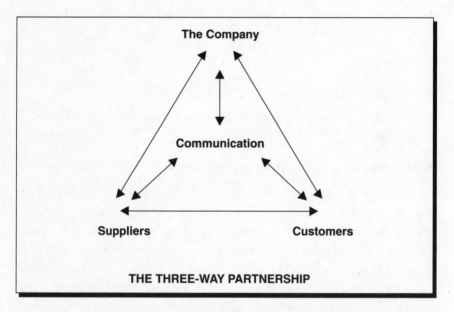

THE THREE-WAY PARTNERSHIP

An example of this is shown in the following case of an Ohio-based process automation design and manufacturing company.

BAILEY CONTROLS

This organization has an extremely close relationship with two of its main electronics suppliers, Montreal-based Future Electronics and Arrow Electronics, headquartered on Long Island.

Future Electronics is hooked into Bailey via a real time data-interchange system. Each week, Bailey sends Future its latest rolling forecast of the materials it will need for the following six months, so that Future can manage its own inventory more efficiently. Bailey itself stocks only sufficient inventory for a few days' trading. Whenever a bin of parts falls below a designated level, a Bailey employee laser scans the bin's bar code into the data system instantly alerting Future of an immediate need for restock. (This is a good example of an electronic Kanban system in operation.)

Arrow Electronics is plugged into Bailey even more tightly. It has a warehouse in Bailey's plant, stocked according to Bailey's twice-monthly forecasts. In this case, Bailey provides the warehousing space and Arrow a warehouseman plus the half-million dollar inventory.

In the other direction, towards Bailey's own customers, its relationship with paper manufacturer Boise Cascade is a model of the new-style customer-supplier partnership. Both Bailey and Boise Cascade share information and expertise to ensure that issues of quality and technological improvement are aired openly and resolved beneficially. For using Bailey exclusively, the eight out of ten Boise plants that signed into the partnership receive a predetermined discount on equipment and engineering services. Regular business reviews ensure that the terms of the agreement constantly reflect market conditions, and this in turn helps to protect both companies from being hurt by the unforeseen.

Listening to their customers' needs, investing accordingly, and then supporting the investment by a dedicated training programme has certainly paid dividends in the following organization.

IDEAL HARDWARE

UK computer distributor, Ideal Hardware, has built up a £45 million-plus turnover in seven years. Managing Director James Wickes believes this success is directly due to a scrupulous customer-care policy. This includes monthly audits, a dedicated customer-care team of nine and a 90-minute, *daily* training programme – equivalent to 20 per cent of the sales force's time. Customer support offers a 24-hour, dedicated distribution service and an electronic catalogue, developed specifically from research into customers' needs.

▶

改

> The investment in management time and money which these initiatives represent is huge, but James Wickes believes it makes good economic sense.
>
> He says, 'Our staff turnover has been less than 1 per cent in the last four years. This is because our people know we are developing their fullest potential, which leads to enhanced sales.'
>
> Ideal's customer-led policy means goods ordered at 7pm will be delivered the following morning, without the expense of a courier service. Warehouse personnel are trained to understand the fragile equipment they handle. The company receives 1000 phone calls an hour, so each member of the office staff has an answer phone to ensure calls are returned without clients having to queue. Even the packaging has removable labels to save retailers the expense of repackaging goods.
>
> Ideal has invested in a 24-hour, modem-linked information service, which customers can access through their own PCs.
>
> Wickes says, 'Technical questions can be answered without using a phone or fax. That is easier for clients and frees our own internal resources.'
>
> Ideal's newest customer ordering aid is *Profile*, an electronic catalogue on compact disk, the first of its kind, and an idea that came from the firm's monthly phone survey of its 4000 customers.
>
> Wickes adds, 'Our approach makes financial sense because if you invest in customers, they will invest in you.' His clients agree: more than eight out of ten consider Ideal's service is the best in its sector.

THE ENABLEMENT EQUATION
Part 2 – Training

Training in customer care should never be reserved only for specifically designated staff, a 'one shot' event, given sporadically or conducted in a contextual vacuum.

Training for all. I have mentioned before how important training is for all in customer care, not just because this is one of Kaizen's maxims but also because it is essential to the effective introduction and delivery of any worthwhile customer-service initiative. A direct comparison is training only a few employees in time management: they might leave the course knowing far more about it than anyone and be competent to apply their new knowledge, but if no one else understands the necessity for it or is able to apply the same knowledge and skill, they can end up as voices crying in a wilderness – personally enabled but overwhelmed by indifference.

Indifference, lack of understanding, silence due to no one communicating the service policy strategy, inaction due to lack of training – all this can be the consequence in some quarters of *selective* training. Naturally, such consequences will undermine internal customer relationships between the trained and untrained, internal processes and procedures and the provision of external customer care. The effects of a weak link in the customer service chain will inevitably work their way through to end users. Therefore, it is of paramount importance that *all* employees – from the janitor to the CEO – are initially trained (during the same period) in the mission, policy, strategy, objectives and core practices of customer service. Then everyone will pull on the same end of the rope – and know the reasons why.

Multiskilled training has proven to be the vital ingredient in the success of the relatively unknown small Daiichi hotel in Japan.

DAIICHI HOTEL ANNEX

This hotel in Tokyo has shot to the top of the 1994 Nikkei Trendy Index (a regular and highly respected survey of hotels which ranks them according to their facilities and services), thanks to its flexible staffing policy.

The Daiichi Hotel Annex (DHA) scored almost maximum marks in the category of customer service, outdoing such well-known names as the Imperial Hotel and the Okura Hotel. DHA's manager attributes this to the hotel's system of multiskilling for its staff. Instead of training staff for just one narrow specialist job (receptionist, concierge, etc), all staff are grouped into three major service function teams – the room team, the eating and drinking team and the cooking team. The members of each team are trained in all the skills covered by the team's area of responsibility. The room team, for example, is responsible for reception, maid services, concierge services, billing, etc.

▶

▶

The theory behind DHA's approach is that, as hotel life is full of all sorts of unpredictable events, irregular work flows and unusual customer requests, if each employee is trained for only one job, there will be many occasions when the hotel fails to meet customers' needs. If staff are trained for several jobs, work can be shared at busy periods and a complete service can be offered to customers at all times.

Nikkei Trendy staff, for example, made several unusual requests while they were assessing the hotel during their survey. They asked where they could find a colour copy shop, whether some typing could be done for them between midnight and early the following morning, to let them know as soon as a fax was received, etc. All of these requests were complied with by the first person who was asked.

The hotel has a training manual which all employees are well-acquainted with, but a considerable time during induction is devoted to persuading employees of the value of providing an all-round excellent service, in which they cover, when necessary, for their colleagues. Staff should never say or imply, 'That's not my responsibility'. A baseball analogy is used to stress that all bases always need to be covered by someone.

DHA's sudden appearance at the top of the Nikkei Trendy league table has been taken extremely seriously by other major hotels in Tokyo. Many of them are now studying the DHA model.

Continuous training. Any football coach, sales manager, Regimental Sergeant Major, theatre director, bellhop captain knows that a winning team is the result of continuous and consistent training plus conscious and dedicated effort by the individuals. Yet many business leaders presume – despite the striking importance of customer satisfaction to profit – that a single course will suffice for a year or more. Nothing could be further from the truth!

Employees should be trained and retrained at a rate directly proportional to a mix of the frequency, regularity, intensity, quality and responsibility of their contact with (external and/or internal) customers, and to the needs of their job.

The reasons for such an emphasis on customer-care training are:

- the eroding effect of customer contact on self-confidence, morale and skill is more pernicious than often supposed

- a training course is a tangible demonstration of a company's commitment to customer service

- knowledge, skill and especially attitude need constant reinforcement to (a) keep employees consciously competent and (b) maintain parity with customers' demands, power and the legislation designed to empower them

- corporate culture and mission must be made manifest – through training, amongst other vehicles – for them to mean more than concepts to employees

- internal customer relationships need training or coaching support to maintain harmony

- employees need to learn how to work in and use the resources of a team

- employees need information, plus opportunities to share experiences and ideas

- willpower alone, in the absence of training, may be insufficient to maintain focus on the mission/strategy, and personal performance.

The duration of each periodic course is appropriate to its frequency (see Figure on page 104) – *provided the participants have previously attended a foundation core skills course*. For instance, each daily session for direct customer-facing staff need be no more than, say, 30 to 60 minutes; and for a weekly session no more than one or two hours. And because of their regular frequency neither of these sessions needs be a wholly structured event; rather, they can be informal and discussive team meetings themed around, for example:

- exchanging information

- specific customer-encounter problems

- how a particular complaint was handled

- a published article or news item

- a new training film

- new product literature

- a new team member

SUGGESTED FREQUENCY OF REINFORCEMENT CUSTOMER CARE TRAINING

Time per:	Direct Customer Facing	Support	Team Leaders Supervisors	Business Development	Production	Department Managers
Six months +					1 day	2 days
Six months				1.5/2 days		
month		1 day	1.5/2 days			
week	60 mins					
Day	30 mins					

STAFF

Direct Customer Facing	Support	Team Leaders Supervisors	Business Development	Production	Department Managers
Customer service team, receptionists, product demonstrators, service engineers, sales team, product merchandisers, new employees company truck drivers, security personel.	Secretaries, accounts, team, administrators, personnel, team, marketeers, technical support engineers, quality control team.	All group leaders	Materials purchasers, project developers and contractors, commercial developers and business advisors, distribution controllers, PR and advertising team	Production planners, assembly line employees, product designers and developers; plus site and building maintenance engineers, warehouse staff, cleaners; plus computer operators and programmers	All department or division heads, managers, controllers; plus the cEO and the top team

- new corporate market research
- performance statistics
- job rotations
- cross-functional collaboration on standards or problems
- presentations from other departments
- this week's/next week's visitors to the company

The longer duration courses will need structuring, though they too can benefit from themes and informality.

Unstructured or not, all training carries a financial cost that must be accounted for, and like all customer-service initiative costs the costs of training for all (what has been called a 'soft end' cost) must be provided for at the time the 'hard end' costs (electronic and telecommunications hardware, procedural reorganization, customer comfort facilities, etc.) are budgeted in year one.*

More than this, however, training in customer care should be a distinct item in the governing policy and in the year one budget: if training is merely passed over and its costs are included in an existing (albeit 'bumped up') *overall* training budget (or worse, in the marketing or personnel budget) where they will compete for suitable appropriation against other training costs, it is possible that training in customer care becomes compromised by underfunding. This can have a serious knock-on effect in year two and beyond, when new training budgets are based not on what *could* or *should* have been spent on customer-care training (had there been no other competing calls on the available spend) but rather on what was *actually* spent (because, perhaps, the fund intended for customer-care training was absorbed into the general training budget and used to other ends.) Thus customer-service training is reduced year-on-year when, in fact, it should grow in-line with the success of the customer-service initiative and the consequent increase in customer contact. *A reduction in training is not consistent with Kaizen's philosophy of continuous improvement, in this case of personal knowledge and skills and interpersonal and inter-team relationships.*

---

* It is revealing that the amount invested annually in training by UK companies is 1 to 2 per cent of turnover, compared to the 4 to 6 per cent invested by Japanese companies.

改

In other words, the raw question is : Does the customer-care policy determine and drive a specific customer-service training budget or, is it how a general training budget is used that determines how successfully the policy is implemented?

Training in context

Training in customer care must relate directly to corporate mission:

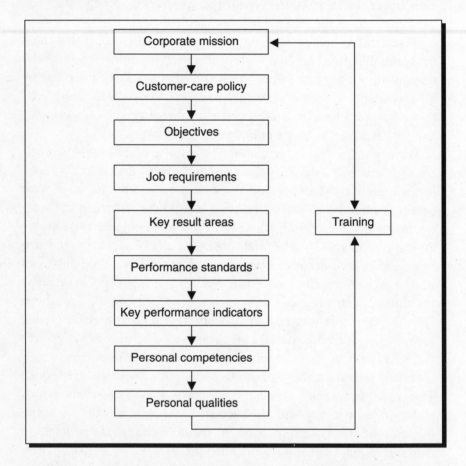

In other words, personal training (on- or off-the-job, formal or informal, one-to-one or group coaching) must bear a straight line – what is known as a canonical line – relationship to what the company has set out to achieve. This not only puts customer-care training firmly in the context of a specific corporate policy but also demonstrates that achieving the strategic aim depends wholly on employee enablement.

THE ENABLEMENT EQUATION
Part 3 – Motivating

Enough about the classic Western theories of people's needs at work and employee motivation has been written elsewhere for it not to be necessary to repeat it here. Suffice it to say that people go to work for a variety of reasons, their expectations differ, and different aspects of work and its rewards motivate people differently. What is common and invariable, however, is each team leader's responsibility to know each employee's needs and to provide opportunities and support for them to be satisfied.

This, though, does *not* absolve individuals from all responsibility: theirs is to take advantage of provided opportunities by participating in, for example, training and education programmes, Kaizen groups, workteam projects, suggestion systems, cross-functional collaboration and information exchange. The fact that this is so actively encouraged in Kaizen companies distinguishes them from other organizations where such a total approach to employee motivation (and development) is largely unpractised.

Unipart and Pedigree Petfoods (a Mars Group company) acknowledge both the job and social sides of their employees. In the former, the Unipart University provides opportunities for staff to develop skill and knowledge in both work and leisure pursuits, and the Constant Learning and Information Centre (CLIC) facility at Pedigree's Melton Mowbray headquarters offers the same chances to get out of work more than a pay packet. Motorola, too, sponsors its own University which operates in four countries, using staff from the Northwestern University Kellog School of Management in Illinois, USA; the Université de Technologie de Compèigne in France; the Asia Pacific International University in Macao; and the University of Edinburgh.

The bottom line of employee motivation is this: demotivated staff will not respond to customers with the right mental attitude, and this is a certain way of derailing a customer-service initiative.

改

THE ENABLEMENT EQUATION
Part 4 – Empowering

It is a poor investment in money, effort, time and materials to inform, train and motivate employees and then withhold the ultimate mark of respect and trust in them, empowerment. As one delegate on a recent training course said, 'This course is necessary, useful and interesting, but I have to ask myself "Why?", because the opportunity to express my new knowledge and influence the way we do things is virtually nil.'

Empowering employees is not to hand them company command and control – that, and ultimate decision-making authority, must remain with senior management (plus shareholders) – but it should enable them to make and act on local decisions which influence their own work. This means that each employee and each team must be given a defined arena of functional freedom within which they can exercise their knowledge and skills. Decisions or actions which potentially take an individual or group across their arena boundary will, of course, be subject to team leader or management sanction, and this will be understood by the employees. But inside the arena the team must be free, that is empowered, to operate according to its own sanctions.

Of course, giving employees this power, albeit on a local scale, requires four things of managers:

1 Confidence in themselves to manage *by exception*.

2 Confidence and trust in their team members to use their empowerment beneficially.

3 Continuous dialogue to reinforce the company culture, values and style.

4 Leadership that reinforces the company mission to provide first-class customer care.

The result of empowering employees is conscious and observant attention to detail and improvement. Some examples of empowerment in action at Marriott International include:[7]

---

7 E . Fuller (see Note 8).

- a guest at a Marriott hotel lost some coins in a drinks vending machine, so he asked a cleaner who was passing how he could report the broken machine. Without hesitation the cleaner put his hand in his pocket, gave the guest a refund, and promised to report the problem immediately, which he did. His manager reimbursed the money

- two businessmen were to have a meeting over lunch at a Marriott hotel, though they were not staying at the property. While walking to the hotel, they were caught in a heavy downpour, and arrived at the hotel very wet. Rather than sitting uncomfortably in the restaurant, staff at the hotel arranged for a guest room, room service lunch and bathrobes. Their clothes were dried and pressed while they had their lunch in private

- a guest at a Washington DC area Marriott hotel was invited to join President Clinton on his morning jog. The guest had not anticipated this, and did not have a tracksuit or suitable footwear. It was late in the evening and the shops were closed, so a member of staff lent the guest his tracksuit, and brand new running shoes. Suitably attired, the guest joined the President early the following morning.

In summary, empowering employees is:

- trusting them to make the right decisions, giving them the freedom to do so and ensuring they accept accountability, but ...

- ... assuring them it is all right to make mistakes as long as they learn from them and modify future behaviours accordingly

- legitimising considered risk-taking and pushing down decision-making authority to the lowest level that risks are considered

- establishing clear lines of support, and managing by exception.

改

ODAKYU DEPARTMENT STORE

Merchandizing is crucial to successful retailing and nowhere more so than in Japan, where superb presentation and packaging is the norm. It was thus a revolutionary decision by the management of the Odakyu Department Store to replace outside specialist contractors seven years ago with an in-house team **which had no previous display experience**.

Conventionally, department stores hire professional contractors to do their merchandising during closing hours. Odakyu has reversed this process by forming an in-house Visual Presentation Performance (VPP) Team, formed from existing staff who are seconded for two years and trained to become display experts. They carry out their work in front of customers, dressed in a special uniform of black trousers and red shirt. They gradually transfer their skills to other staff during their tenure in the team so that, when their secondment is completed a new team is fully ready to take over.

The motivation behind this change was threefold:

1 To enhance human resource development by broadening staff skills.

2 To reduce the cost of outside contractors, which before the change was costing the store £35,000 a month.

3 To stimulate other staff to appreciate display as an important sales tool, as opposed to mere decoration.

The VPP Team consists of 21 female staff with an average age of 24. It carries out its work each Wednesday on a two-week cycle: one week it creates new merchandizing displays and the following week it reviews and modifies those displays and plans new ones for the following Wednesday.

Once a month the VPP team brings in an outside display expert who visits all the departments and advises on modifications that might improve visual impact. When the scheme was introduced, departmental managers complained of staff shortages at crucial times, particularly during bargain sale periods. However, this has now been overcome due to the enthusiasm and motivation of staff and by developing internal resources.

Summary

- The enablement equation, Communication + Training + Motivation + Empowerment, produces employees who can think, decide and act critically. Enablement means creating an ethos where it is normal to respond positively to customer-service needs, irrespective of job tasks and function.

- It might be necessary to *deconstruct* old attitudes and behaviour, to create the right open and accepting context for a new culture, before embarking on a major and company-wide programme of staff development and empowerment.

- Communication serves more purposes than informing employees about the content and intent of a customer care policy; it also:

  - reinforces understanding of the corporate paradigm
  - engenders openness
  - promotes involvement
  - motivates
  - enables
  - reinforces identity with a team
  - maintains focus.

A team leader in a Kaizen company *must* be a first-class communicator.

- Communicating with customers and suppliers is just as important as communicating internally.

- Training in customer care must be for all employees, continuous and in the context of corporate mission, policy and commercial objectives.

- Motivating the whole person – taking a holistic approach to individual development – is more effective than motivating the person just for work.

- Enabling means fostering the responsible use of initiative and personal judgement in deciding what is an appropriate and reasonable level of customer care.

7

RESEARCHING
THE
MARKET

INTRODUCTION

S ome manufacturers do seem to know what consumers want; some confidently influence likes and dislikes to the extent that they determine our wants for us. These companies have a distinct advantage because they have information which their competitors do not.

Good market research forewarns manufacturers and suppliers: it enables them to prepare and plan – to forearm – with precision, and it prevents wasted effort born of 'market myopia'. Research reduces manufacturing and pricing risks to manageable odds.

However, any form of market research is only as good as first, the method employed; second, the extent, detail and honesty of the data collected; third, the regularity with which research is conducted; fourth, how truly representative of a total population is any sample of respondents; fifth, how expertly the collected data are analyzed; sixth, how willing the company is to share the results and conclusions internally; and seventh, how willing the company is to respond to the conclusions.

These points are illustrated in the following interview. It illustrates something of how a large national organization, a bastion of tradition, is beginning to take note of its own customer research and to change – albeit slowly – to create products and a service which its customers want. It has sometimes proved a bitter pill to swallow; but nevertheless, the BBC has decided to involve its licence payers (its customers) and its programme makers (its suppliers) very early on in the decisions made about what products (the programmes) its listeners and viewers will receive. The watchwords in the BBC today are its *accountability* - to its customers - and satisfying *customers' needs*.

THE BBC

Feedback is a weekly programme on BBC Radio Four devoted to listeners' queries, suggestions, comments and complaints about the BBC's output on all five of its national radio networks. The programme is an independent production presented by Chris Dunkley, the *Financial Times*' radio and TV critic. He speaks during the programme on behalf of listeners. On January 20, 1995 Chris Dunkley interviewed Michael Stevenson, Secretary of the BBC. As Mr Dunkley explained, Mr Stevenson's 'function is to form a bridge between the Board of Governors and the Board of Management, and to be responsible for the BBC's business administration and its accountability.'

Mr Dunkley introduced the interview by reminding listeners that they had raised concerns about the BBC's accountability (to its listeners) in the previous series.

What follows is an edited transcript.

Chris Dunkley   '... you said that public opinion was already vigorously monitored: how is public opinion vigorously monitored by the BBC?'

Michael Stevenson   'The programme strategy review, which is all about what schedules we will have over the next five to seven years, has been grounded in an exhaustive interrogation of what audiences are saying to the BBC. But at the Governors' level we've put in place a new complaints process – the Serious Programme Complaints Unit. (We have a licence payers' database enabling the Governors to understand what the audience in their masses are really saying to the BBC.)

'We've put in place Governors' seminars that try to get at those difficult issues of public interest in broadcasting – only last week we published an account of the first seminar on how the BBC should go about reporting crime. And let us not forget the wide range of public meetings, one every week, where the audience has a chance to interrogate BBC managers. All of those new measures lead me to believe the BBC is very carefully monitoring opinion.'

Chris Dunkley   'After I've interviewed BBC executives on *Feedback*, listeners often write to me (saying) they sound over-defensive and autocratic. Just one example, after my interview about Radio 3 in our last series, (a listener) wrote and said, "I was astonished

▶

改

▶ at the arrogant and patronising response to complaints from the audience." That's absolutely typical of the letters I receive after (similar) interviews. What people are saying is, "You always tell us (that) Auntie knows best."'

Michael Stevenson 'You wouldn't deny the BBC's right to put its case fairly clearly whenever it's under assault. From time to time, I pick up that old arrogance which I associate with public schools in the 1950s, and when I do I jump up and down, and I think all my colleagues do as well.'

Chris Dunkley 'Over and over again people write to me in resignation, it seems, or disgust saying that they've tried every avenue, they've done what they've been told to in terms of addressing the BBC, and they're convinced that all this accountability business is sheer PR and that even *Feedback* itself is just a valve where people can harmlessly let off steam. What do you say to that?'

Michael Stevenson 'If accountability were a valve, PR, then I've been wasting my last two or three years. As I see it, it isn't changing the BBC's fundamental mission, but it is changing the way in which the BBC expresses itself and makes clear to the public at large, which pays the licence fee for the services, what it thinks it's up to, how it changes its mind when it does change its mind and what it's going to be doing over the next five years. That is not PR; it is getting clear inside the mind of the place what it's for and how it does its business.'

Chris Dunkley 'Could I finally put to you a letter which takes a rather different stance? (A listener) reckons it must cost the BBC a million pounds a year – that's his arithmetic – just to answer letters from the audience. He thinks that amount of money may be difficult to justify. He thinks letter writers may be taken *too seriously*. And he says, "The small minority of articulate listeners who write letters or phone the Duty Office are probably unrepresentative of listeners as a whole; yet broadcasters, desperate for instant feedback to their programmes, tend to give more weight to letters and phone calls than to the Audience Research department's interviews with a representative sample of listeners. Thus the articulate middle class – always ready to pick up the phone or pen a telling letter – have a grossly disproportionate influence on BBC policy." What do you think of that?'

Michael Stevenson 'I think there's a real point beneath what he says. There is a danger that the BBC is in constant correspondence with quite a small group of its viewers and listeners, who are articulate and feel strongly and elicit a reply from the BBC. I've been talking to you about how much the BBC goes on from there to take into account a much broader swathe of view and opinion, understanding the whole of our audience in all its complexity and sophistication.'

Reproduced with the kind permission
of Brian Lapping Associates Limited
and the BBC.

The BBC has been compelled by legislation, economics and the pressure of public opinion to change – not only its broadcast output but also its culture and its management, programme commissioning and production processes; but more than this, it has come to understand that it *must* respond to the market research data it invests many thousands of pounds in each year if it is to retain its customers through giving them the programmes, service and customer satisfaction that the data says they demand. A problem with which the BBC, like other large 'labyrinthine' organizations, has to contend is persuading the many internal groups – many motivated by self-serving and competing interests – that enhanced customer service is *the* measure by which listeners and viewers judge how well their licence fee is being used. What the BBC should not forget, however, is that customer satisfaction is the product of *six* Satisfaction Elements: its accountability – a factor of the Culture Element – is just one of them. Nonetheless, the BBC is beginning to change its air of superiority by getting closer to its customers, even eliminating the barriers so that a partnership between them can be established. In February 1995 the BBC published its new strategy document, *People and Programmes*.

Getting closer to customers

In a *Harvard Business Review* article in 1994, the authors wrote:[8]

---

8 F.J. Gouillot and F.D.Sterdivant, '*Spend a Day in the Life of Your Customers*', Harvard Business Review, Jan/Feb 1994.

改

Top-level managers need to spend a day in the life of key customers. There is no substitute for managers' instincts, imagination and personal knowledge of the market. It should be the essence of corporate strategy. Only in that context can analytical devices like customer-satisfaction indices, market-share data and bench-marking results become servants rather than masters. And only with market-focused leadership can companies continuously and quickly reinvent themselves to meet new market needs.

This very much reflects the Kaizen approach of *keiretsu*, forming a network of alliances with customers (and suppliers). The closer these ties are the more likely will they develop into mutually – supportive relationships, in which a constant dialogue can significantly help the supplier produce what it knows its customers want, and customers will know that what they buy will fulfil their expectations.

The key to the profitable success of these relationships is to forge them between the staff in the supplier's organization who have the authority to influence production and supply and *all* the staff in the purchasing organization who are involved in the purchase decision. Take, for example, a commonplace illustration: when selling a new car to the prime user in a married couple the salesperson should also develop a relationship with his/her partner, whose influence on the purchase can be crucial. The married couple is obviously not a 'purchasing organization', but it is a simple Decision-Making Unit in which both people's opinions are important even though probably only one of them has the 'authority' to agree the purchase.

A DMU is a group of individuals who influence or are influenced by a buying decision. In industrial organizations they are generally the staff with the:

Money — the individuals who administratively control a purchase budget

Authority — the individuals who determine where the budget will be spent, and who have 'signing off' power

Need — the individuals who will use the purchased product.

These people are the ones to whom a supplier must get close for they are the customers, and it is their individual and collective needs and preferences which are important and about which information must be gathered – the fundamental question being, what do they want? There are many ways of finding out.

RESEARCH METHODS

The following is a list and brief explanation of the ten most common methods of researching customers and markets.

Personal meetings by a company executive – essential (as the HBR article suggested), but as the meetings are likely to be sporadic and cursory the inadequacies of such personal sampling must be balanced by data gathered by other means.

Customer panels – a customer panel consists of a number of people who reflect the typical profile of a market segment, acting as a company's 'guinea pigs.' Their perceptions and opinions as test customers considering a broad range of issues is a valuable source of subjective data.*

Customer focus groups – a productive way of identifying customers' opinions about a specific issue. These small group – intensive and facilitator – led question and brainstorming sessions can be highly revealing, but as they concentrate on only a narrow horizon they can be a time-consuming and expensive way of gathering data statistically relevant in depth or breadth. However, the results can provide useful pointers which the company can choose to validate by other means.

Critical incident analyses – these require staff, skilled in non-threatening interrogative techniques and in report writing, to record customers' feelings when they have been particularly pleased or displeased by service received. The written report must be classified (under an 'incident type') and used to stimulate action, to justify the exercise.

---

* Ford's new compact car is the first to have involved women throughout its design stage. The Women's International Marketing Panel – (WIMP) (!) – sits with about 20 regular members from 12 of Ford's European markets. The panel includes secretaries, managers and engineers. Other women are invited to specific test clinics – focus groups – on particular aspects of design.

Customer interview videos – by its nature, this method also is likely to be time-consuming, expensive and limited by personal sampling. However, the advantage of capturing interviews on film is the chance it gives to also analyze body language – hence the emotional content – in conjunction with the interviewees' verbal responses.

Mystery shoppers – these are people contracted to a company to be its 'sensory representatives' in the field, and trained to record their experiences objectively as a real-life customer. Mystery shopping is an invaluable source of actualité data and is a common way of gathering mass information cost-effectively.

Market research – **market** research data give only half the story, **customer** research data give the rest. There are significant differences between how these two sets of data should be used. Market research measures customers in groups and gives aggregate – or macro – results aimed at helping a company determine customer base – influencing strategies.

Customer research emphasises the micro – the individuality of customers – and aims to influence a company's *internal* satisfaction processes.

Customer comment (and guarantee) cards – a passive way of collecting information. As the number of customers who are prepared to fill out a response card is likely to be only a small percentage of all customers, the data might not be statistically relevant. Again, however, some issues – which might need deeper probing – can be revealed. The response rate can be increased by simply making the cards visually appealing and by attaching an incentive to their completion. But it must be borne in mind that some people will return only a positive comment because they believe they will not receive their reward for a negative one.

Opinion/Perception surveys – conducted as either face-to-face, telephone or postal interviews, these surveys are a useful way of actively gathering mass information. They can, however, suffer from what has been called ' interviewee inertia', that is the state of boredom and indifference caused by being asked to respond to yet another questionnaire. Therefore, interviewers must be trained adequately, the questionnaire must be designed expertly and the exercise must be funded properly to ensure a sufficiently robust set of data.

Product user groups – are useful forums from which to capture implementation/application opinion and, frequently, modifications which real customers have designed and find increase value-for-money. The key is for the manufacturer to link with the groups without appearing to take them over or use its association for ulterior and hidden reasons. Trust and openness can produce a genuine two-way flow of data.

Using more than one research method

Obtaining regular and substantial feedback from customers is crucial to positioning the company and its products precisely. It is a common and false assumption that just one or two feedback methods are all that are needed to get a clear, and continuing, picture of customers' needs and opinions. Many companies know that a single communication channel will be wholly insufficient: as every research method inherently contains its own unavoidable potential to corrupt the quality of data, they tend to use all means of feedback to smooth out the anomalies caused by single processes. The sheer wealth of resulting data can be overwhelming (and the cause of another set of problems to analyze it), but it does allow the simultaneous correlation of macro and micro information to inform strategic (executive) and tactical (operational) decisions.

The bottom line

Japanese companies are more inclined than those in the West to share research results widely – the team and communication networks encourage this. The tendency in the West is for ownership of results to be expressed proprietorily by the department which commissioned the research, and this prevents their circulation to others at a time when the company should be reacting quickly and *in concert* to get full value from its investment in the research.

改

ROLLS ROYCE MOTOR CO.

The prestige car manufacturer Rolls Royce has reaped many benefits from its introduction of 'Strive for Perfection' its TQ programme based on Kaizen.

Among the changes which have taken place has been a thorough programme of employee education. Included in the policy of inform-ing employees has been an unusual idea to make sure employees know what customers think of their cars.

Regular research is conducted on behalf of the company among owners of Rolls Royce and Bentley motor cars, and a written copy of the results of this research is made available for each team to see. In addition, cassette tapes are made of customers' comments. Employ-ees can take these tapes away and listen to them, for example in their own cars. The system has proved popular and has supported other initiatives to enhance understanding between customers and employees.

There is, after all, only one reason for investing in customer research and a culturally-based customer-care initiative – improving the bottom line. It is not enough to do either blindly, merely to improve image or because competitors are doing it. A company must derive a positive cost-value benefit from its investment; that is, the research and initiative costs must be exceeded by an increase in sales value due to improved customer satisfaction. (This might take time to feed through, and it is not necessarily a straightforward process to relate customer satisfaction efforts to the bottom line. But if through cus-tomer satisfaction volume and revenue can be influenced by 1 per cent, profits can be levered by 10 to 15 times.) Similarly, a customer's cost-value analysis must show a positive balance: the value of the ser-vice they have received must exceed their raw costs of purchase. (This means putting a financial value to them on factors such as quality, delivery and every other aspect of the entire satisfaction package.) Clearly, a cost-value analysis provides an opportunity to identify and act on those satisfaction (and dissatisfaction) factors that will posi-tively impact trade with each customer, hence the bottom line.

ENCOURAGING CUSTOMERS TO RESPOND

A problem which every company experiences is encouraging customers to respond to any research method. Customers must have a good reason for doing so. Response motivation can be enhanced by creating a relationship in which potential respondents feel that their comments are genuinely valuable and will be actively considered; that they will ultimately benefit from improvement suggestions; that the research process will not be too intrusive or lengthy; and that their views and any disclosed personal details will stay confidential. Observing these criteria will build trust and confidence and an environment in which respondents are more likely to give full and honest answers. It will also encourage a *partnership* – perhaps the most productive and mutually beneficial liaison that can exist between a supplier and its customers.

PARTNERSHIPS

'The Customer is King' is a shibboleth that today only reminds us of the rather unsophisticated and saccharin smile campaigns of the 1980s. It quickly became a cliché, a somewhat empty slogan that few companies really respected for it implied the question, If the customer is King does that make us, the supplier, a servant? No one in business wanted to be, or saw themselves as, a servant or, by inference, inferior. Suppliers now realize that they too must be Kings – of product quality, and supply and service – to be able to serve customers 'regally'. Equality, where neither customer nor supplier is jockeying for superiority at the expense of the other, is the product of the increasingly common co-operative relationship between both parties. In such relationships – 'learning relationships'* – companies

---

* Establishing learning relationships with customers depends on four inter-related strategies, according to Pine, Pepper and Rogers in their March-April 1995 Harvard Business Review article. These are, an *information* strategy for promoting and managing dialogues with customers; a *production/delivery* strategy for customizing products according to customers' preferences; an *organizational* strategy to ensure an appropriate fit between company and its customer environment; and an *assessment* strategy for evaluating performance and responding to feedback.

have found that the *prevention* of complaints, product rejection, debilitating price wars and lost business is much less expensive than cure after the event; and customers have found that being able to rely on the availability of high-quality products which *they* want, at a fair price from trusted and ethical suppliers which also provide first-class service is much more reassuring and time-effective than taking a purchase risk – and, perhaps, having to complain or seek redress as a consequence.

CANON (UK) LTD

The photocopier sales team at Canon's Leicester Branch Sales Office were, like the teams elsewhere and those in other manufacturers, heavily incentivized on new business. Having sold a machine, it was in a sales person's financial interest to quickly find a new customer. Existing customers were therefore rarely proactively recontacted or revisited until just before the expiry of their lease agreement, which could amount to a three-year gap between contacts.

Steve Norman, Canon's Regional General Manager, saw an opportunity to close a potentially fatal customer-care gap and build a bond with customers. He built into the post-sale administration process a courtesy-and-research phone call one week after each sale. The research element sought answers to how well each stage of the sales cycle – from initial contact to machine delivery and user-staff training – was handled. The courtesy element involved establishing a relationship between the Canon interviewer and the principal machine operator in the client company, to ensure a direct and clear channel of communication that allowed the customer to seek help quickly and Canon to provide value-added service and sales. The most significant impact internally of this approach was felt by the sales team, who saw the sales administrators as key internal customers whose new role would have a marked influence on repeat sales.

Getting to the stage where a partnership is feasible can take an enormous amount of effort, honesty and trust – starting with a commitment from both sides to make the transition from the familiar form of confrontational, short-term market trading to one based on new rules of long-term mutuality, where neither side is 'king'. Strategic partnership discussions between *commercial* customers and suppliers

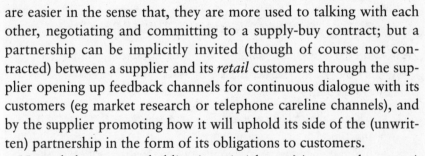

are easier in the sense that, they are more used to talking with each other, negotiating and committing to a supply-buy contract; but a partnership can be implicitly invited (though of course not contracted) between a supplier and its *retail* customers through the supplier opening up feedback channels for continuous dialogue with its customers (eg market research or telephone careline channels), and by the supplier promoting how it will uphold its side of the (unwritten) partnership in the form of its obligations to customers.

Nevertheless, a set of obligations (a 'charter' in any other sense) does not mean that customers will be locked-in for evermore. I have written earlier how a charter can be as empty and meaningless as the slogan 'The Customer is King': as customers' cost-cutting and service improvement hunt is on-going, suppliers must back up their promises in-depth culturally so that their apparent interest in understanding and responding to customers' needs is made visible by every employee at every level in the company. This is what customers will respond to and what will keep them buying from one supplier rather than another. Remember, being a customer does not come with a job description.

Lord Sheppard, Chairman and group Chief Executive of Grand Met, has said, 'Customers are increasingly looking through the front doors of the companies they buy from. If they do not like what they see in terms of corporate culture, social responsibility, community involvement, equality of opportunity, they won't go in.' It seems, therefore, that partnerships must be culturally-driven, and should exist not only between individual customers and suppliers but also between suppliers and the wider socio-ecological environment to which their customers belong; in other words, if a supplier cannot relate beneficially to its social community it might not be given the chance by the individuals within it to relate to them: they could take their business elsewhere.

改

THE CO-OPERATIVE BANK'S ETHICAL POLICY

Following extensive consultation with their customers with regard to how their money should be invested the Co-operative Bank's ethical policy states that:

1 It will not invest in or supply financial services to any regime or organization which oppresses the human spirit, takes away the rights of individuals or manufactures any instrument of torture.

2 It will not finance or in any way facilitate the manufacture or sale of weapons to any country which has an oppressive regime.

3 It will not encourage business customers to take a pro-active stance on the environmental impact of their own activities.

4 It will actively seek out individuals, commercial enterprises and non-commercial organizations which have a complementary ethical stance.

5 It will not speculate against the pound using either its own money or that of its customers. It believes it is inappropriate for a British clearing bank to speculate against the British currency and the British economy using deposits provided by their British customers and at the expense of the British tax payer.

6 It will try to ensure its financial services are not exploited for the purposes of money laundering, drug trafficking or tax evasion by the continued application and development of its successful internal monitoring and control procedures.

7 It will not provide financial services to tobacco product manufacturers.

8 It will continue to extend and strengthen its Customer Charter, which has already established new standards of banking practice through adopting innovative procedures on status enquiries and customer confidentiality, ahead of any other British bank.

9 It will not invest in any business involved in animal experimentation for cosmetic purposes.

10 It will not support any person or company using exploitative factory farming methods.

11 It will not engage in business with any farm or other organization engaged in the production of animal fur.

12 It will not support any organization involved in blood sports, which it defines as sports which involve the training of animals or birds to catch and destroy, or to fight and kill, other animals or birds.

Summary

- Research overcomes 'market myopia' and reduces operational risks to manageable odds.

- Effective research is dependent upon:

  1 Method.

  2 Extent, detail and honesty of the collected data.

  3 Regularity/frequency.

  4 Statistically relevant sampling.

  5 Expert analysis.

  6 Data sharing.

  7 Willingness to respond to the conclusions.

- A supplier's customers are all the people involved in a purchasing Decision-Making Unit. These are the people to which it must get close, and about which information must be gathered.

- Research methods can be classified as:

改

	Active	Passive
	Market Research	
Macro	Mystery shopping	Guarantee cards
	Opinion/Perception surveys	Coupon redemption analyses
	Customer Research	
Micro	Personal meetings	Customer comment cards
	Customer panels	Product user groups
	Customer focus groups	
	Critical incident analyses	
	Customer interview videos	

- The more channels of feedback (research) used the less likely will data corruptions, the potential for which is inherent in each individual channel, be incorporated uncorrected into analyses.

- Customers must have a good reason for responding to research requests. They must feel that, for example:

  1 Their comments are genuinely valuable and will be considered.

  2 They will ultimately benefit from improvement suggestions.

  3 The research process will not be too intrusive or lengthy.

  4 Their comments will remain confidential.

- Co-operative relationships between supplier and buyer are increasingly common. It is one of Kaizen's maxims that a strong three-way relationship should exist between a company, its customers and its own suppliers.

- Today's customers also expect companies to enter into an equally strong socio-community-ecological partnership that demonstrates its social responsibility.

8

BUILDING LONG-TERM RELATIONSHIPS WITH CUSTOMERS AND SUPPLIERS

改

INTRODUCTION

In January 1995, Tesco launched *Clubcard* into all 500 of its stores. Clubcard has been called a customer-loyalty programme. Describing the scheme as a 'way of thanking customers for shopping at our stores,' Sir Ian MacLaurin, chairman of Britain's second largest supermarket group, said card members could accumulate points redeemable against money-off vouchers. The voucher discounts would amount to £20 per year if a customer spent about £50 a week – the average. Tim Mason, Tesco's marketing director, echoed the store's advertising slogan when he said, 'It doesn't sound like much (the discount), but every little helps.' The scheme will enable Tesco to learn more about individual customers, in particular how frequently they shop, which store they use and their preferred products. It is estimated that to cover the 1 per cent discount on offer Tesco will need a sales uplift of some 5 per cent. It is likely the national roll-out of Clubcard will cost Tesco upwards of £50m in its first year.

In a nutshell, Tesco's Clubcard scheme reflects the pros and cons of so-called loyalty programmes:

Pros

- customer incentive and motivation to demonstrate purchase constancy
- chance to build long-term relationships
- marketing opportunities
- competitive edge
- increased sales
- customer research data
- Foundation for tie-ins to additional offers.

Cons

- the difference between a loyalty programme and an incentive programme
- set-up costs
- on-costs which must be covered by attracting increased sales
- reward(s) which might not be sufficiently motivating to win long-term loyalty
- redemption processes which might be too complex for customers
- the time and money it would take an average customer to accumulate sufficient points for a worthwhile reward
- loyalty can be to the incentive rather than the supplier, which could mean loss of business once the programme ceases.

'LOYALTY' OR 'INCENTIVE'?

Despite the (potential) downsides of establishing a loyalty scheme many in UK retailing are immensely successful – Barclaycard's *Profiles*, Esso's *Tiger Tokens*, *Air Miles*, Homebase's *Save and Spend* and Benson and Hedges' *Gratis Points* are good examples. However, while a loyalty scheme is *not* a substitute for such core values as product quality and customer service it can attract customers who might *then* be willing to test how well their needs are met and they are treated beyond their 'mercenary' motive and the supplier's marketing motive. This brings into question whether a scheme is designed to reward true loyalty or to lure customers indiscriminately with an incentive.

Of course, it is not only retail companies that can benefit from offering a loyalty scheme, though commercial and industrial suppliers seem not to pay sufficient attention to developing loyalty among their key customers. A 1993 survey of 100 leading UK companies by

P-E International, the management and computer services group, found that most of the respondents did not know what is required to build customer loyalty. The survey report said satisfied customers feel good only as long as their current needs are met and only as long as they perceive that a supplier is giving value. *Committed* customers want more than a transient bait: they want to develop a long-term strategic relationship with a supplier which understands and responds to their individual needs, and which discriminates between customers who have been *genuinely* loyal over a period and newcomers who have yet to demonstrate an allegiance.

This means the supplier ascertaining what customers want, ranking these needs in the form of a satisfaction index and then re-engineering to build genuine loyalty-generating processes and activities. A mix of personal interviews, sales feedback and research questionnaires will help a company construct its customers' satisfaction profiles, and from these a 'performance improvement planner' (*see* Fort Saunders below). This simple SWOT-type matrix not only highlights those factors which will have the greatest impact on customer loyalty but, because the factors are those identified *by customers* as important to them, it will also close the perception gap which often differentiates a supplier's and its customers' opinions of the quality of service provided and wanted.

FORT SANDERS

Fort Sanders Health System is a six-hospital group based in Knoxville, USA. To develop appropriately it took an outside-in approach, allowing its customers to advise it how to re-engineer to maintain and build loyalty.

Each quarter over a year and a half 1200 former patients were telephone polled to develop a customer-service index. Patient focus groups were used for more detailed sales and service feedback. After six quarters of research the database included nearly 8000 individual satisfaction profiles. From these, 34 key and common factors were distilled to create a universal satisfaction index ranked according to factor importance to customers. The factors were then transferred to the four quadrants in a SWOT-style performance improvement planner, which clearly showed where Fort Sanders should focus its development activities to improve customer satisfaction and build loyalty.

What the research found was it would cost the hospital group very little to improve those factors ranked highly by patients. The performance improvement planner, continuously up-dated by new research, governs the work of cross-functional improvement teams and the group's training department.

Fort Sanders' Performance Improvement Planner

	1 Primary Opportunity Areas	**2 Primary Maintenance Areas**
High ↑		
	Invest resources here	*Maintain high standards here*
Loyalty Impact	**3 Secondary Opportunity Areas**	**4 Secondary Maintenance Areas**
↓ **Low**	*Investment is needed here, but quadrant one has priority*	*Changes here will have little impact on satisfaction and loyalty*

Low ◄——————— Customer Satisfaction ———————► High

The reason a loyalty scheme can be a highly valuable addition to a customer-care initiative is simple: it is easier and less expensive to retain existing customers and important to keep key customers than to attract new ones. Loyal customers tend to spend more compared to promiscuous ones whose loyalty has not been won. But, as I stated earlier, a loyalty scheme cannot be a surrogate for real customer service; neither can it be a me-too add-on: it must be integral to a company's fundamental business strategy and its customer-care mission.

Writing in 1993 about the American credit card company, MBNA, Frederick Reichheld, a director of Bain and Company, said, 'MBNA (a 'loyalty leader' in its field) are successful because they have designed their entire business systems around customer loyalty. They recognise that customer loyalty is earned by consistently delivering superior value. By understanding the economic effects of retention on revenues and costs, loyalty leaders can intelligently reinvest cash flows to acquire and retain high-quality customers and employees. Designing and maintaining this self-reinforcing system is the key to achieving outstanding customer loyalty.'[9] He went on to say, 'The forces in a loyalty-based system are cumulative. The longer the cycle continues, the greater the company's financial strength. At MBNA, a 5 per cent increase in retention grows the company's profits by 60 per cent by the fifth year.'[10] MBNA's customers are loyal to the company and stay with it for the service and personal attention new customers get from the beginning and the incentives which can be earned for *long-term* custom.

9 F.F. Reichheld, Director of Bain and Company, writing a *'Loyalty-Based Management'* in Harvard Business Review, March/April 1993.
10 Ibid.

AIR MILES

Frequent flyer schemes were initially introduced by domestic airlines in the USA during the early 1980s. At the beginning of 1990 airline carriers out of America started to introduce the concept.

British Airwarys started its UK scheme in 1992, a year after it launched a frequent flyer scheme in America. The Executive Club Scheme now covers 49 countries around the world, and some two million members, half a million of them in Britain.

This is almost modest by the standards of some American schemes, which run into many millions, but, according to Sarah Newman, general manager of relationship marketing for BA, there is a distinct reason.

'The American schemes have very different criteria for membership. We are really trying to reach the regular traveller, to reward loyalty and to talk to them all the time about what they need. We listen to customers a lot, by letter, or by asking them in small groups, and the Executive Club is an ideal way to maintain that relationship.'

In the past, BA has flown Executive Club members into the UK from as far away as Japan to talk about how they view standards of service, and what new facilities they would like to see the airline introduce. The most spectacular result was the introduction of Club Europe last year. The search for a new European class began in 1992 when a group of 80 flyers from around Europe were flown to the UK to spend a weekend talking to BA staff and senior marketing officials about what would make the ideal business air-travel service.

The travellers were looking for a service that was more European and less British, they wanted more space in the air and less waiting on the ground, and they needed more flexible fares. From the interviews, BA was able to profile its average European customer much more accurately than would have been possible using older techniques, such as clipboard interviews in terminals.

改

THE RIGHT CUSTOMERS

A loyalty scheme can reward either all customers indiscriminately, or just some, in which case the question is, which ones? Clearly, whether the target population is everyone or a selected proportion they should be the 'right' customers; that is, right for the business strategy. If the target population is chosen correctly it is likely to be fairly homogeneous (or divisible into homogeneous segments), and their common needs will enable the company to adjust its whole offer package to serve them properly and economically. Knowing which customers are the right ones, those who are or are likely to be loyal, also identifies those which are not because they are likely to defect. As Reichheld wrote, 'Cable television companies talk about increasing retention rates but then recruit new customers via price promotions and free sampling – techniques that draw out of the woodwork precisely those customers hardest to keep. Those recruitment efforts merely load the pipeline with people who are inherently disloyal.'[11] This somewhat dismissive view of 'legitimate' marketing activities nevertheless hints at two conundrums. The first is that suppliers cannot afford not to keep finding new customers, and such fairly non-arbitrary promotion tools play a useful role in raising awareness, interest and motivation in potential purchasers. Suppliers know they will experience some customer loss once the promotion period ends, yet their hope is that enough customers will stay not only to cover the costs of the promotion and the costs of administering customer acquisition – and pipeline loss – but also to grow their base of retained customers who, by definition, are likely to be the long-term loyal customers which they need. This is a self-pruning process that sorts out the promiscuous from the stable. What Reichheld is saying is that self-selection is not as economically efficient as more precise initial targeting: the inherent waste (anathema to Kaizen organisations*) in a blanket approach draws off resources which should be used to retain and, importantly, reward just those customers who by every demographic, socio-economic and satisfaction index measure

---

10 *Sunday Times*/Unisys Customer Care Pull-out, 11 June 1995.
11 *See* note 9.
* The Japanese dislike overheads and indirect costs intensely. Anything that does not contribute directly to a company's products or relationships does not add value.

are actually or highly likely to be loyal customers even without the magnet of a special offer: their magnet will be the Satisfaction Elements, and confidence that their individual needs will be met.The second conundrum takes me back to my earlier question: when is a loyalty scheme a real loyalty programme and not a marketing-driven incentive scheme for an undifferentiated population? Surely, price promotions, free sampling, tokens, points and special offers are, as I referred to them above, examples of product or supplier marketing designed to attract new customers (or waiverers) and retain their business via inducements? Their loyalty to the supplier rather than the reward is yet to be determined. Thus, shouldn't a loyalty programme more properly reward long-standing or key customers who deserve a personal thank you for their *proven* length of association or importance to the business strategy?

These customers are the 'right' customers and, given that they will form only a proportion of a supplier's total customer base at any one time, shouldn't a loyalty programme be selective, for major customers exclusively? Defining a loyalty programe in this way suggests that Tesco's Clubcard is not one; it is more an incentive scheme whose true impact on customers' loyalty *to Tesco* will only be found once the scheme ends.*

It is perhaps no coincidence that Clubcard was marketed nationally to coincide with the activities launched by Sainsbury to celebrate its 125th anniversary. This is not to discount the value of such schemes – they are popular, but by the same token the Fort Sanders programme *is* a real loyalty programme in that the only incentive is a medical service designed by customers for customers. Their loyalty is to the supplier, not a free offer. Winning whole-hearted and lifetime loyalty is thus determined by providing superior value, relationship opportunities and fulfilment of customers' needs.

The success of a mission to provide superior value can be measured by its first -, second -, and third-order effects:

---

* Tesco's Clubcard seems to be a high attractor: in April 1995 Tesco overtook Sainsbury for the very first time to become Britain's biggest food retailer.

改

1st order effect   – customer loyalty (quantified by retention rate and fulfilment of estimated lifetime value)

2nd order effects – revenue growth (the result of repeat purchases and referrals)

　　　　　　　　　 – declining costs (the result of lower customer acquisition expenses plus the efficiences of serving known customers)

　　　　　　　　　 – increased employee retention (the result of higher job satisfaction and better rewards due to enhanced productivity)

3rd order effect   – increased profit.

As Reichheld says, 'Unless managers measure and monitor all of these economic relationships, they will default to their short-term, profit-oriented accounting systems, which tend to focus on only the second- and third-order effects. Focusing on these symptoms – instead of on the primary mission of delivering superior value (service) to customers – often leads to decisions that will eventually reduce ... loyalty.'[12]

A classic example of this, one from which many lessons were learnt, concerns Green Shield stamps in the UK. By the late 1970s every type of retail outlet was offering them. Soon double stamps were being given, then triple, then quadruple until ten- and twentyfold stamps were available. Customers shopped wherever they could get the most stamps for their money. There was little loyalty and a great deal of chasing the incentive. Retailers failed to provide any form of customer care, and when the Green Shield Stamps enterprise collapsed many suppliers discovered the real object of their customers' loyalty.

Incentives are just one of the factors from just one of the six Satisfaction Elements. They alone will not engender loyalty, particularly if a competitor offers a bigger and better incentive and this is a prime purchase motivator. An incentive scheme can be a powerful attractor,

---

12　*See* note 9.

but as the recent television advertisement for Direct Line, Britain's largest direct motor insurance company, says, 'People come to us for the price but stay because of the service.'

MEDWAY PAVILION SERVICES

Medway Pavilion Services is situated about halfway between London and Canterbury on the M2 motorway. Since 1993 the Medway service station group has initiated a customer-loyalty programme, not unlike Fort Sanders', aimed at increasing staff focus on customers. The range of activities designed to improve internal communication and outward-looking action includes:

- a range of restaurants
- an exchange bureau for overseas visitors
- local decision-making involving employees' suggestions
- promoting employee involvement in the business
- active stimulation of customer feedback
- a new staff newspaper
- shop staff who are asked to record in a special, personal notebook any item which a customer asks for which is not on sale
- continuous training, coaching and encouraged empowerment
- making each service station feel like a comfortable and fun place to be, rather than a convenient place to use the toilets.

改

SUPPLIER PARTNERSHIPS

In many business areas, of paramount importance alongside relationships with customers are good long-term relationships with suppliers. The practice of manufacturers getting to know, supporting, and in some cases even assisting in managing, first-tier suppliers is common practice in Japan, and has been followed by many of the Japanese manufacturers who have set up business in Europe and the USA. Nissan in the UK, for example, has close relationships not only with its suppliers but also with its suppliers' suppliers.

Increasingly, Western companies are also fostering these relationships, in order to enhance the quality and reliability of their own products and services.

ROTHMANS

During the 1980s, Rothmans used to buy its stationery from a number of suppliers which the company played-off against each other to drive down the purchase price. However, to ensure the continuous availability of stationery and off-set the risk of supply or quality interruptions (a situation it had created for itself), the company had to hold large buffer stocks. The professional relationship which Rothmans formed with a single supplier in 1989 saved the company many thousands of pounds a year and the need for its warehouse, and gave the supplier guaranteed orders at a fixed price. Their partnership encouraged both parties to openly discuss quality, delivery schedules and service in a risk-free environment of shared responsibility.

Summary

- A loyalty scheme should never be a substitute for core quality and service values.

- A so-called loyalty programme may, in fact, be an incentive programme designed more to lure customers and reward them *before* allegiance has been established than to reward them for loyalty once it has been proven.

- Committed customers – those who are loyal to the supplier rather than a transient bait – want a long-term relationship with a supplier which:

  1 Enters into a strategic partnership.

  2 Understands and responds to individual needs.

  3 Acknowledges genuine loyalty.

- Loyalty-building processes and activities must be based on thorough customer research.

- Winning whole-hearted and lifetime loyalty is determined by the quality of service, fulfilment of customers' needs, relationship opportunities – plus provision of all Satisfaction Elements.

- Long-term supportive relations with suppliers, and even with suppliers' suppliers, brings huge benefits in terms of quality and greater customer service.

9

THE TECHNOLOGY TO IMPROVE CUSTOMER SERVICE

改

INTRODUCTION

Electronic Data Interchange (EDI) is an increasingly common feature of supplier/customer partnerships. EDI automates such processes as order taking and administration, and enables customers to monitor the status of their orders directly and in real time. It therefore quickens order placement and fulfilment and can eliminate entirely the time-consuming and expensive paper-based systems of old. EDI underpins computer-driven Kamban systems.

'Customer Intimacy' (USA) or 'Channel Partnership' (as it is known in Europe) aims to go beyond EDI in its classic order processing role, by using technology to open up pathways to, and support person-to-person relationships with, customers – both corporate and individual. CI/CP is made possible by the new telesales systems software which is fast enough to bring a customer's details on to any operator's screen instantly once any one of a number of simple file identity and access codes has been accessed by a software platform or keyed-in, and which is versatile enough to capture file updates as the customer/operator conversation is unfolding.

The technology should always be a tool within a customer-service operation, never the master. Writing in a May 1994 Unisys-sponsored *Sunday Times* Supplement on Customer Care, Chris Partridge quoted Jonathan Harker, a senior associate with the business consultancy CSC Index, who referred to three rules for successful channel partnerships. These correctly sandwich technology between satisfying customers' needs and managing customer service profitably:

'First, fulfil customers' requirements, and customize your product or service to meet (their) needs.

'Second, manage your marketplace. You need to be (good) at database (management) so that you can be more selective about who you want to be intimate with.

'Third, it is no good implementing a customer-intimacy programme if it loses you money.'[13]

In other words, the technology is *relatively* useful: a CP database in itself is no more than an information repository that needs constant updating with information from direct contact with real customers (the data wellhead) to prove its currency, and the software is no more than a carrier whose operational usefulness is dependent upon its ability to cope with the dynamic realities of partnership trading with real people.

DELL COMPUTERS

As an instance of what I mean, the telephone management technology at Dell, the direct marketing PC manufacturer, was designed with two objectives in mind: to improve the company's already established customer-support services, and to reduce the service operating costs. Its European sales and support operations are centred on its computerized telephone system at Bray, a village on Eire's coast to the south of Dublin. The Bray team of 250 multilingual operators handle on average 6000 calls a day, each of which is answered within an average of ten seconds. It is the quality of its installed technology that, Dell believes, enables it to provide the sort of personalized and individual service (an 'intimate' service) that generates the customer loyalty on which its business has grown.*

---

13 *Sunday Times*/Unisys Customer Care Pull-out, 15 May 1994.
* Dell Computer Corporation is one of the world's top five computer companies, and the third largest in the UK, with annual revenue approaching $3bn. 75 per cent of Dell sales are to existing Dell customers. Dell sells to over two thirds of the *Fortune 500* US companies and to over half of the UK *Times Top 100* companies. Michael Dell, founder of the company, was named 'Entrepreneur of the Year' by INC Magazine in 1989 and 'CEO of the Year' by *Financial World Magazine* in 1993. The company says it talks directly to 50,000 customers worldwide every day.

改

CUSTOMER CARELINES

As the technology and the idea of channel partnerships has developed, so have carelines (or helplines). These are the current growth area in customer service. They are a means of providing a convenient and easily accessible gateway into a company, and a way of its responding immediately and demonstrably to customers' queries and complaints; yet until some seven to ten years ago, in the UK, the benefit of direct contact with customers that a telephone number provides was overshadowed by the worry of what giving open access to customers could mean. However, UK companies have been influenced during the intervening period by the helpline culture in the USA and Europe (France and Germany, especially) and are now beginning to introduce contact numbers more widely and, as they are finding, to their advantage; indeed, companies here seem to be generally more advanced in the way carelines are used, being far more administratively geared up to feed into internal databases and the internal service chain the information generated from in-bound calls. Perhaps it is the immediacy of a telephone call that lends an urgency to this information over and above that generated by a more distant and time-consuming piece of market research.

Nonetheless, the potential cost of establishing a careline service plus a still widespread belief that a careline will be used predominantly as a 'grouseline' still exert a brake on its faster growth. But Coca-Cola and BurgerKing, for example, who print an 0800 (toll free) number on their soft drinks and carryout bags in the UK, have found that their customers' calls (over 150,000 annually, in Coca-Cola's case) cover every conceivable issue from minor to major. Overall, Coca-Cola find that the calls they receive are a good barometer of public opinion which, additionally, forewarn the company of impending issues which could become sufficiently important to warrant corporate attention and active intervention to resolve long before they could hurt the company.

A careline need not be expensive to establish – particularly if its cost is balanced against the direct and tangible benefits which can be generated versus those derived from, say, a poster campaign. As part of a company's customer service a careline is becoming increasingly essential. Customers want the comfort and opportunity of relating to real people in the manufacture of their bought products – an illegible signature of some unnamed and uncontactable person, at the foot of a standard and xeroxed letter, is simply no longer good enough.

At anywhere from £500 to £5000 a careline service can be tailored to suit the needs and budget of every company; and it need not be a service built and manned in-house: it can be contracted out to a tele-marketing agency which has already invested in the physical space, technology and staff training. As far as careline callers are concerned, they should never suspect that an agency is acting as intermediary.

As careline advocates know, it pays to be able to receive and react to queries, complaints, suggestions and opinion immediately, profes-sionally and efficiently: there is a high correlation, for instance, between a complainant whose problem is managed quickly and their consequent willingness to repurchase, and equally between com-plainants who cannot conveniently vent their emotion and their readiness to take their business elsewhere – and persuade many others to do the same. There may well be an expense involved in establishing and maintaining a careline, but the value of being able to 'get intimate' with customers and thereby retain their existing custom is priceless.

So, too, is the sheer value of in-coming information to learning, adapting and continuously improving – the actions on which Kaizen is predicated. The phrase *asset management* comes to mind: in this context the asset is a company's customer base and management of it is made more effective with the help of technology plus current infor-mation – whether this is gathered via a formal market/customer survey or informally via the *vox pop* responses to a careline number.

SYSTEM FACILITIES

The advent of integrated computer and telephony systems – Com-puter Aided Telephone(y) Systems (CATS) – enabling, for instance, to know who is calling and to bring up on screen the history of their association with the company before answering an in-bound call, is transforming careline and direct line selling services. Calling *L*ine *I*dentification (CLI or CLID) and *C*omputer *T*elephone *I*ntegration (CTI) are the acronyms used to describe these facilities.

The information which can be passed on to an operator's screen by a CLI/CLID facility can consist of a number of elements:

- the caller's own telephone number and, if appropriate, their business's name
- the caller's name
- the date, time and elapsed duration of a call
- information on the caller held in the receiving company's database (for example, their purchase and payment record, copies of correspondence, synopses of general enquiries, faxes, etc).

By the time the in-bound call is answered all this information can be displayed in front of the operator, enabling them to respond to the caller by name and with full reference to their profile with the company. The profile can be presented in text or graphic form according to, perhaps, the department in which an operator works, eg an operator in sales might prefer profile information in the form of bar charts, while a colleague in accounts perhaps prefers the same profile in a numerical format on a spread sheet. (If no database information is available, the operator can complete a screen-based file in real time as the call unfolds and the customer's details are gathered.) 'Personalized answering' – another term for CLI/CLID – is becoming increasingly common.

Enhanced signalling interfaces, such as Integrated Services Digital Network (ISDN), Primary Rate Access or Digital Private Network Signalling System (DPNSS) are needed to allow personalized answering to calls received via public or private networks. The market prices of the appropriate CLI software and PC terminals for a large business environment will generally be less than a proprietary standard and stand-alone Private Automatic Branch Exchange (PABX) and a suite of feature phone handsets, and the increased benefits of being able to provide a comprehensive and intelligent database-driven careline service will be significant. *Callpath*, for example, is IBM's architectural structure (an 'application enabler') for a family of connectivity and voice processing products. In effect, it is the 'glue' between data processing and pure telephony functions which provides the operating company with a consistent interface.

The figure below illustrates this simply.[14] The application could be any, for example reservations, order placement or a careline/help desk, running on a data system; then there is some enabling software with a defined interface, supported by a PBX and Automatic Call Diverter (ACD). The decision as to which platform to run the application enabler from depends on such factors as where customers' data are held (Remote Database Access (RDA) – might be required), where the phone system is, where the telephone operators (telephone agents) are located, where the call centre is situated (for example Dell Computer's European centre is south of Dublin), and how much data are moving.

To illustrate the advantages that an integrated system can bring, consider a traditional teleselling or helpline operation. In-bound calls will be answered by a plain greeting, followed by the obvious but very necessary caller-identification questions: Who are you? What do you want? Do you have an account reference number? and so on. Once this information is given the caller might then be rerouted to a more appropriate operator (to whom the caller might have to repeat his or her details), or handled by the original call receiver; but in any event the caller's details will first be typed into a computer (in full or via single keystroke commands) before any information on them held in the company's database can be brought up on screen. Thus there are effectively two separate conversations going on: the voice conversation between customer and operator and the computer conversation between the operator and the database. The two conversations in this scenario are integrated manually by the operator. What a product like *Callpath* does is provide integration at the technology level. Needless to say, a CAT system overcomes the guaranteed customer loser – 'I'm very sorry, I don't have your file in front of me. Can you call back in an hour?'

cx

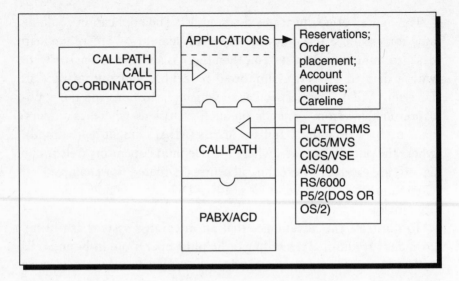

A more sophisticated careline system, then, will be integrated with the operating company's computer system.

The range of facilities – functions – which such a system will offer can include:

Intelligent answering. This brings up on telephone operators' screens any available data on the in-bound caller before their call is answered so that the operator can greet the caller by name and intelligently by reference to the on-screen profile information.

'Intelligent answering' includes Dialled Number Identification Service (DNIS), CLID and Automatic Number Identification (ANI).

Co-ordinated voice/data transfer (VDT). This permits screen-based data on a customer to be transferred simultaneously with the transfer between extensions of their in-bound call. For example, a customer calling a motor dealership for new car prices might also want to book in their current car for a service. Using VDT, the new car salesperson can transfer the call with the customer's vehicle service history to the service department.

Consultation. This is a variation of VDT by which a telephone operator can either transfer screen data to his or her supervisor for advice while keeping the customer on hold, or include the customer in a three-way conference while the operator and supervisor refer to the same customer information on distant screens.

Intelligent dialling. This facility automates out-bound calling. For example, at the end of a working day a company can 'down load' trading information to each of its branch offices (including those overseas) or to its field representatives or teleworkers. On-time computer assisted call back is another example of intelligent dialling.

Personal services. A term which covers the automation of many inter-office dialling functions all of which, for example call transfer or setting up conference calls, can be initiated by a single programmed function key and a single keystroke.

Call data reporting. This facility enables the production of management reports on the productivity of the system and of individual telephone operators.

An interface to a neural network. This facility can help an operator by, for example, intelligently planning despatch loading and shipping of an urgent order for a customer.

An interface to advanced function printing. This enables a supplier to tailor the design of its despatch notes and invoices to suit the individual requirements of each customer. For example, the position of bar codes could be critical to their automated scanning at the customer's premises.

A simpler system might be voice-based only (Voice Enhanced Applications (VEA)), still allows customers integrated access to a wide range of information. The facilities available can include:

- *Modular design.* This allows the system to be enlarged in modular increments, with appropriate disk storage options.
- *A platform for multiple-voice applications.* This feature permits concurrent execution of different voice processing applications,

改

such as voice response, voice messaging and voice facsimile.

- *Voice recognition.* This permits customers to use a limited vocabulary to interact with the system. It also permits customers with rotary (analogue) telephones to access the system.

- *Text-to-speech.* As the feature term suggests, this facility converts text information to be spoken to a caller using computer-generated synthesised speech.

- *Multiple-language support.* This enables voice messages to be carried on the system in the languages appropriate to the community which the company serves, and selected by in-bound callers.

Summary

- The technology should always be a tool within a customer service operation, never the master. It has to be paid for and it must add value to the bottom line: there is no point in being the best technology-served customer-care company if the company goes broke in winning the accolade.

- Customer intimacy is becoming more common and, as it does so, customers' threshold of service expectation is being raised. Those companies which can offer channel partnerships have a significant competitive edge – to which the increase in direct line selling (of insurance and financial services, for example) is ample testimony. However, nothing can replace a genuine feeling for customer service: a CAT system will not make an excellent service team from uncaring, disinterested, apathetic operators – it will merely speed up the process of turning customers away.

乙メ

THE HIGHLIGHTS

CHAPTER 1

Why Customer Care Needs Kaizen

Window 1

Many customer care programmes have not been based on fundamental changes. Kaizen can provide that framework.	A Kaizen approach can discover the root causes of customer dissatisfaction and help to introduce improvements.
A Kaizen approach involves everyone in the company, as well as customers, suppliers and other stakeholders, in improving the business – and increasing customer satisfaction.	Kaizen makes customer care a natural and never-ending process.

Window 2

Comprehending the superficial or immediate causes of customer dissatisfaction is usually easy – they are mostly obvious.	In Kaizen companies, the response to a customer complaint is twofold: first resatisfy the customer; that will rectify matters from their point of view. Second, discover the *real* cause of the dissatisfaction.
This means asking two questions with relentless persistence: What did *we* do wrong? and Why? Eventually the ultimate cause(s) of the problem will be found and put right to ensure it does not recur.	Just because a problem comes to light at the supplier-customer interface does not mean that that is where the problem originates. Very often the cause lies deep in the company – a long way from the point of sale; but if every employee accepts a responsibility for customer care, even those far from the front line can contribute to the prevention of customer dissatisfaction.

改

CHAPTER 2

Kaizen

Window 3

Kaizen means – and requires – continuous and gradual process improvements, and the elimination of anything which does not add value to what customers buy.	The overarching aim of Kaizen companies is *profit through quality products and services leading to total customer satisfaction.*
Kaizen promotes the idea of advancing via many small evolutionary steps rather than a single revolutionary quantum leap.	Kaizen is an entire culture system, described by its ten principles. Each should be adapted to a Western business culture, introduced carefully (perhaps only one or two at a time) and observed by every employee but especially by team leaders

Teams and Team Leaders

Window 4

One of Kaizen's tenets is, get the management process right and the wanted results will follow naturally and inevitably.	Team leaders in Kaizen companies are primarily communicators, motivators, educators, para-psychologists, and culture/values role models.
Workteams and team autonomy are the foundations of corporate structure in Kaizen companies. In the West, it is likely that individuals and teams will want more autonomy and creative freedom than their counterparts in Japan are generally permitted.	Team meetings – plus the time and venue for them – are an inseparable and indispensable part of process-oriented management. It is said of Kaizen companies that one + one = three.

善

CHAPTER 3

Kaizen's Instruments

Window 5

All Kaizen's instruments are human centred. In Kaizen, simple is best. Each instrument should be both a symbol of Kaizen and a signpost directing conduct towards the fulfilment of customer satisfaction. Not all instruments are useful to developing a customer-care culture and programme. These are the instruments of greatest direct value to a customer-care programme:	Other statistical and group tools: – Pareto analysis – fishbone diagrams – brainstorming, etc.
– Process-Oriented Management (and Visible Management) – Cross-functional Management – The PDCA Cycle. – Suggestion Systems – Kaizen Groups (the successor to Quality Circles).	Again, it is important that Western business leaders bear in mind the greater *personal* autonomy employees in the West expect. Suggestion Systems and Kaizen Groups, for example, have been described as means of coercing Japanese employees to conform and defer to *group* consensus. This can compromise personal initiative.

改

CHAPTER 4

Excellent Customer Care

Window 6

ISO9000/BS5750 is of less importance to Kaizen companies, other than the importance attached to it by the customers and suppliers with which they deal. Of far more importance are the internationally-recognized quality awards such as the Deming and Baldridge Awards.	All six Satisfaction Elements must be developed and delivered concurrently. The Elements are universal; their Factors are relevant to the customer and markets served.
Of the six Satisfaction Elements, the Culture Element is the most influential; it is the driver behind a company's values, ethics, style, standards of performance, relationships, conduct and the behaviours expected of employees. Kaizen is a powerful cultural force.	Customer Charters will be hollow documents unless they are underpinned by a positive culture that unites *all* activities and *every* employee in the pursuit of customer satisfaction. Remember, nothing will have changed, in spite of a Charter, until customers perceive a change. Kaizen is a route to perceptible change.

CHAPTER 5

Breaking Down Internal Barriers

Window 7

A company's top team, senior managers and team leaders, should each dedicate between 40 and 50 per cent of their time in the early stages of a customer-care initiative coaching for improved internal relationships.	Treating colleagues and other employees as internal customers contributes substantially to the achievement of excellent external-customer care.
Internal customers have rights and corresponding responsibilities: the quality and style of these relationships should mirror the standards of relationships formed with external stakeholders.	The service chain is wholly dependent upon the interactions between the people working in a company. Every employee's work contributes to a branch, or the main trunk, of their company's service chain.

改

CHAPTER 6

Motivating and Enabling Employees

Window 8

Enabled performance is the consequence of Communication + Training + Motivation + Empowerment. In Kaizen companies training is, perhaps, the most important and formative tool, for training inherently contains elements of communication and motivation with the objective of enabling the delegates and creating a knowledge-based culture.	A Company's mission is the contextual framework onto which the activities in an employee-enablement programme must be designed to add the 'tactical' flesh.
Communication – communicating externally (with suppliers and customers) is as important in Kaizen companies as communicating internally.

Training – this must be for all employees, continuous and in the context of mission, customer-care policy and (KPIs) Key Performance Indicators. | *Motivation* – the classic Western theories of motivation and the satisfaction of people's needs at work should still inform the process of management in a Kaizen company in the West.

Enablement – each team should have its own arena, within which it is free to act according to its own sanctions and initiatives. |

CHAPTER 7

Researching the Market

Window 9

Good market research forewarns: it enables companies to prepare and plan – to forearm – with precision; and it prevents wasted effort born of 'market myopia'. Research can reduce commercial risks to manageable odds.	A company must get close to all the people in its customers' DMUs; these will be the people with the money, the authority and the need.
No single research method by itself will give a clear, continuing and non-corrupted picture of customers' needs and opinions. As many channels as possible should be employed to smooth out the anomalies caused by single processes.	Market research gives a macro picture; customer research gives a micro picture. Both are required to inform strategic (executive) and tactical (operational) decisions.

改

CHAPTER 8

Building Long-Term Relationships with Customers and Suppliers

Window 10

A loyalty programme should reward customers who have proven their loyalty to a supplier; an incentive scheme tends to be less discriminatory.	A loyalty programme can never be a substitute for core quality and service values, driven by corporate culture and exemplified by employee attitudes and behaviours.
Committed customers – those who are loyal to the supplier rather than an incentive – want a long-term relationship (a strategic partnership), by which their needs will be understood and fulfilled.	Close relationships with suppliers are vital to enhance quality and, ultimately, customer satisfaction.

CHAPTER 9

The Technology to Improve

Window 11

Technology should be used to improve customer care and the profitability of providing service. It is, in other words, the means to an end, not the end itself.	A careline (a telephone helpline or service line) is a convenient and easily accessible gateway into a company, which offers direct person-to-person/company contact.
'Customer Intimacy' or 'Channel Partnerships' enable a company to manage its customer-base asset more effectively, by learning from, adapting to and improving via incoming information.	Carelines are becoming an increasingly beneficial and important channel of communication.

The highlights in the eleven windows above underscore the Kaizen approach to customer care.

PART III

UNITING
CUSTOMER
CARE
AND
KAIZEN

10

DEVELOPING
AND
IMPLEMENTING
A
KAIZEN-BASED
CUSTOMER-CARE
STRATEGY

改

Three management ideas, (or 'constructs', as I call them), which are currently very much at the heart of Western business thinking – cultural change, the learning organization and strategic planning – include elements which are also very close to the Kaizen approach.

CULTURAL CHANGE

In his book, *Charting the Corporate Mind*, C.H. Turner wrote,

> 'How products are made and designed must, in the end, depend on how the social systems creating these products are made and designed. Lonely, ugly and adversarial relationships will result in badly fitting assemblies of junk that shake apart when used.'

In his 1990 *Camino Lecture* – 'Culture Change: No Science but Considerable Art' – Sir Colin Marshall, deputy chairman and chief executive of British Airways, said,

> '... how do we at BA, as well as in British companies generally, need to address the challenge of culture change and the closely coupled requirement for *changes in underlying values?* (Author's italics)

> 'In a service company, persuading staff and managers that smiling at customers is a good thing is certainly necessary, but it may only reflect

a mode or a fashion .... It may well be a paste-on, a graceful convenience rather than an action indicative of a real shift in values towards or what customers are, and must be, to any service company – the ultimate purpose which selects and determines the priorities of all its activities. The reason so many companies seem to achieve a useful change in culture and then slowly disintegrate over the passage of even short spans of time is that one suspects they confuse the appearance of culture change – the presence of the symbols – with the needed solid change in values, and their acceptance. My point is, it is not just the increments of time and effort which are important, but .... if we accomplish no basic shift in values, if we confuse appearance with reality, then over the long term we will accomplish no real change in the culture at all. Thus for the phrase "culture change" to be meaningful, it has to be time-qualified, and it must be built on a firm base of truly altered value frameworks.'[15]

Speaking in 1991, Michael Murphy, Chairman and Chief Executive of Dublin-based Golden Pages Ltd, reflected on the culture and process changes which he and Bruce Reed, executive Chairman of The Grubb Institute, had steered through Golden Pages:

'1 Traditional training or development fires individuals during the sessions but soon the new ideas are submerged within the company culture. The Golden Pages process is changing the ethos which, in turn, is allowing individuals to grow and expand.

'2 There are no magic answers to our institutional challenges. We have to wrestle with and harness the ordinary. When we do, we come to see the extraordinariness of the ordinary in its contribution to the achievement of institutional objectives.

'3 Changing how we manage our organization is threatening .... It is also empowering.

'4 Lip service from the top to change or a rule book for change designed by organizational specialists, will not create real change, the type of change which will reflect itself in the outputs of our institutions.

'5 Engaging – as we have done – with all employees has thrown up another layer of potential middle managers committed to performing "in role". [*See* the diagram below for an explanation of the phrase "in role".]

---

15 Sir Colin Marshall, Deputy Chairman & Executive British Airways plc, published in *The Proceedings of the Camino Lecture* RSA Journal, Vol. CXXXIX No 5414, January 1991.

'6 Finally, the process as it evolved in Golden Pages enables us to cope with uncertainty and the fundamental changes in our market-place ...'[16]

Bruce Reed added,

'Performance indicators are now available throughout the company so that staff and managers no longer have to ask other people how well they are working. The information is there for all to use. This has three major effects:

- First, knowledge is no longer (exclusive) power since it is now freely available.
- Second, staff can manage themselves. That is, they accept responsibility for their own performance in relation to their colleagues.
- Third, as a result they can take authority for their work and derive satisfaction from that realisation.'[17]

16 M. Murphy, Chairman and Chief Executive, Golden Pages Ltd, Dublin, writing on '*Creativity in Leadership: Middle Managers in the 1990s*', published in the RSA Journal, Vol. CXXXIX, No. 5416, 1991.
17 B. Reed, Executive Chairman, The Grubb Institute, writing with M. Murphy. *See* note 16.

'IN ROLE' RELATIONSHIPS AT GOLDEN PAGES[17]

Old – relying on making personal relationships to get things done. If people fall out with each other the work suffers.

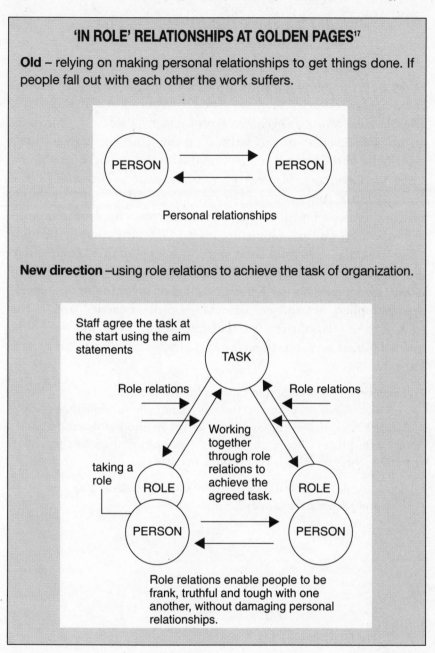

Personal relationships

New direction –using role relations to achieve the task of organization.

Staff agree the task at the start using the aim statements

TASK

Role relations

Role relations

Working together through role relations to achieve the agreed task.

taking a role

ROLE

ROLE

PERSON

PERSON

Role relations enable people to be frank, truthful and tough with one another, without damaging personal relationships.

17 Ibid.

改

THE LEARNING ORGANIZATION

Sir Colin Marshall's view, that more than time and effort are required to develop the paradigm shift towards a culturally-based and motivated customer-care strategy, is echoed by Womack *et al* in their book *The Machine that Changed the World* and by Professor John Burgoyne in much that he has written on the 'learning organization', principally in the book he co-authored with Pedlar and Boydell, *The Learning Company: A Strategy for Sustainable Growth*. In the Womack book, American and Japanese car manufacture is compared. The authors contend that one of the reasons why American auto manufacturers got into (sometimes fatal) difficulties during the mid-1980s to early 1990s was their vigorously exploitative, competitive and aggressive way of relating to their suppliers. They drove them under, as opposed to the Kaizen practice of investing in and developing suppliers as strategic partners – a process carried over in the style of their relationships with customers. Burgoyne, like Sir Colin, maintains that learning organizations sustain excellence over time. He has said:

> 'Many organizations seem to function rather like a drunk going down a corridor. They set off in a certain direction; after a while they crash into the wall; if they survive, they set off in another direction and repeat the process. At best they reach the end very bruised. Change and learning through crisis is very painful and wasteful.
>
> '[A] learning organization veers away from the walls as it approaches them and adapts ... smoothly.'[18]

---

18 Prof. J. Burgoyne, Centre for the Study of Management Learning, Lancaster University, writing on '*Creating a Learning Organization*', published in the RSA Journal, Vol. CXL, No. 5428, 1992.

He used this analogy with a group of managers from British Airways but they said, 'Yes, but in addition the corridor is incredibly twisty and the walls keep moving.' Burgoyne's considered response, which he also offers as a definition of a learning organization was, 'A learning organization continuously transforms itself in the process reciprocally linked to the development of all its members; a learning organization also achieves sustainable development through enriching rather than exploiting its context.'[19]

By this he means enriching employees, customers and suppliers – as well as enriching its social community and the wider ecological environment.

Burgoyne has developed a list of characteristics common to organizations that have learnt to adapt and change to their contexts:[20]

1 *A learning approach to strategy*. This implies that deciding collectively what to do, and implementing it, has itself to be a learning process; that is, (a) considering alternatives from a bottom-up fountain and a top-down cascade of suggestions, (b) choosing a suggestion, (c) piloting it, (d) determining contingency suggestions, and developing them in the event of the prime suggestion failing its trial, and (e) establishing performance benchmarks, monitoring systems and feedback loops to assess and report on the viability and feasibility of the piloted suggestion.

2 *Participative policy making*. Burgoyne cites one of the common observations of Kaizen companies in Japan (and which I have mentioned in terms of its strengths and weaknesses): that proposed organizational moves tend to be discussed in great depth for a long time. Only when a consensus (even a majority consensus) emerges are they piloted, then put into practice. This invariably takes longer than only a smaller, private group determining policy but, as Burgoyne says, 'What you lose on the extra discussion and thinking time you get back on the implementation time.' And, as he also says, the more employees who are involved in policy design the more each team is

19 Ibid.
20 Ibid.

改

prepared for its implementation, contingencies, commitment, ownership and, ultimately, getting it right first time.

3 *Informing: open information systems.* Networking and Information Technology is making companies more transparent. Business leaders should not underestimate the power of available knowledge to transform attitudes and performance, nor the increasing need for it: they can respond in either a closed way by closeting information with themselves on the 25th floor or, in an open and constructive way by disclosing and sharing information to help their people understand, cope, adapt, learn, change and, ultimately, work *together* to achieve corporate objectives.

4 *Formative accounting and control.* By this, Burgoyne means displaying performance information in real time, as the lathe is turning or the assembly line is running, rather than at some point after the event when it may be too late to take meaningful corrective action. Clearly, an appropriate software program is needed if the display is computer based, but the 'paper and pen' approach to SPC in many Kaizen companies can work just as well.

5 *Mutual adjustments between departments.* As organizations become flatter and leaner certain management processes and skills become vitally important as substitutes for the replaced triangular hierarchy, familiar anchor points and, invariably, middle managers. Among these are the need for strong and inclusive teams, horizontal communication and collaboration between teams, visible team leadership, job enrichment (through information and empowerment) to replace upward job promotion – which is more difficult as old layers will have been stripped out – multiskill training to enable lateral movement, and a clear focus on customers to give purpose to roles and goals. All this demands mutual adjustment and understanding.

6 *Reward flexibility.* This means endeavouring to get the kind of rewards and conditions for employees right in a way that reinforces learning. This is very much individual to the culture of each company and, perhaps, to its industry. In Kaizen companies there is a great emphasis on a team approach to work and, consequently, rewards

for, say, ideas contributed to a suggestion system. However, not only are some Japanese companies now adopting Western-style perform-ance-related pay for senior managers, Western employees are more used to receiving personal merit awards for *individual* contributions.

7 *Adaptable structures*. Kaizen teams are by implied definition and actual practice adaptable and this inherent flexibility (through multi-skilling, education, empowerment, task sharing) is carried over into the organization which, it will be remembered, understands that change is endemic and, therefore, that constant adaptation (reinven-tion of itself) to its context is unavoidable.

8 *Boundary workers as environmental scanners*. In his 1979 book *Mind and Nature*, Gregory Bateson defined *systems* as 'activities with a boundary'. And in the 1950s the London-based Tavistock Institute defined managers as 'those who work on the boundary of a system.' Burgoyne implies these definitions by speaking of managers who, as I have stated earlier, should manage only by exception; that is, they should monitor their systems' boundaries and only step in when, for example, a team's activity takes it across the boundary separating its own area (or system) of freedom from its surrounding environment, or when a performance deviation in a system requires corrective action. Burgoyne also refers to employees working at the *corporate* boundary – at the customer/supplier interface – who can scan (or monitor) for market or customer information. Such employees could be van drivers, service engineers, receptionists, careline operators, etc. These direct customer-facing staff are boundary environmental scanners.

9 *Intra- and Inter-organizational learning*. Learning organizations learn from their mistakes, share the learning process and the results of appraising the causes of the error and, importantly, admit the mis-take openly in the first place. They also help the suppliers linked to them in a strategic partnership to learn how to implement the manu-facturing and delivery standards which are required. Nissan, Toyota and Marks and Spencer are companies which have strong paradigm links with their suppliers.

改

10 *Learning culture and climate*. As Burgoyne says, 'a learning organization is likely to have an unwritten rule that says "It's all right to make a mistake once, but it is not all right to make the same mistake two or three times – if you have used your freedom and all the available knowledge and resources wisely and responsibly."'

11 *Self-development opportunities for all*. Self-development logs, self-served learning contracts, self-managed learning budgets and *à la carte* training – all guided, facilitated and resourced by the organization – are signs of a mature approach (that is, less directed, prescriptive or coercive) to employee training and development in a learning organization.

Clearly, there are many similarities between Burgoyne's characteristics of a learning organization and Kaizen's ten principles, as the table below shows.

Kaizen's principles		The characteristics of a learning organization
● Focus on customers	*is equivalent to –*	
● Make improvements continuously	"	● Formative accounting and control
● Acknowledge problems openly	"	● Intra and Inter-organizational learning
● Promote openness	"	● A learning approach to strategy and participative policy making
● Create workteams	"	● Reward flexibility
● Manage projects through cross-functional teams	"	● Mutual adjustments between departments
● Nurture the right relationship process	"	● Learning culture and climate
● Develop self-discipline	"	● Adaptable structures
● Inform every employee	"	● Informing: Open information systems
● Enable every employee	"	● Self-development opportunities for all

STRATEGIC PLANNING

A company must know where it is today (and what it is today), where (and what) it wants to be tomorrow, and the route it must take (how it must change) to reach its goal. So much is already obvious – it is, to use some jargon, a classic 'motherhood' statement! But is such explicit sense consistent with today's need to be ever more transparent and responsive to customers, to operate manifestly open systems, to be a learning organization – in other words, to be wholly flexible and adaptable to omnipresent changes in the marketplace?

The answer is unequivocally *yes*, though matching a 'solid' business strategy to a 'fluid' environment is naturally going to be more difficult than when the environment too is static. In current trading conditions the acid test questions are: Is it possible? Can we do it? For how long will our strategy remain relevant? How much time have we got? Do we have the right resources? What market forces (perhaps beyond the current horizon) might cause us to substitute the strategy (in whole or in part) with a contingency plan?

There is no doubt that strategizing is a gamble: the art is in managing the risk by managing the strategy to ensure its relevancy stays intact. Ultimately, the dominant question is, What do our customers want (or, what *will* they want) and are we prepared to supply it? This is not a question of artifice: its simplicity belies the prime importance of the answer to corporate success. As Kaizen states, profit will be earned ultimately through customer satisfaction.

These three constructs highlight the fundamental building blocks of the aim of this book:

1 Develop the appropriate values framework.
2 Transform the organization to a learning/Kaizen organization.
3 Encapsulate the vision in an encompassing customer-focused strategy.

They also indicate that for many companies the introduction of a Kaizen approach would not be a totally alien process.

The question now is how best to do it?

改

DEVELOPING AND IMPLEMENTING A KAIZEN-BASED CUSTOMER-CARE STRATEGY

There are three core strands to developing a Kaizen-based customer-care strategy:

1 Strategy.
2 Kaizen culture.
3 Customer-care approach.

1 DEVELOPING A STRATEGY

A 'strategy' is a description of how a company will achieve its formal objectives and goals. It translates vision into actions and, via a regular planning and analysis process, states how the organization's resources will be used to gain and sustain competitive advantage and produce benefits for all stakeholders.

The process of formulating a strategy can be shown graphically in the diagram (*see* page 179).

Competitive advantage can be achieved by pursuing either a broadly *cheaper* strategic thrust, where higher profits result from lower prices for the same product (assuming lower prices lead to higher volumes) or, a broadly *better* thrust, where high profits result from higher-added product or service value at the same price (assuming the additional value appeals to more consumers). In either case, greater efficiency plus innovation are necessary supports, as is the marketing aim of convincing customers that their needs will be more fully satisfied by one company's products rather than other competitors'.

However, to be sustainable over time, competitive advantage must be based on unique, non-tradeable and non-imitable strengths, and it might be necessary to build protective 'barriers' around the company and its product(s) – to ward off imitation and attrition – by, for example, 1 ensuring a dedicated organizational fit between the company and its environment, 2 creating a market-responsive corporate culture, and 3 forging strong customer and supplier relationships (strategic partnerships) that can help control access to the supply and distribution channels.

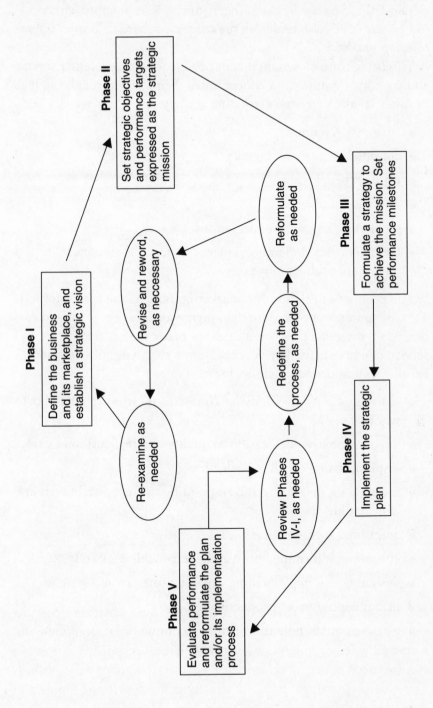

Phase I

Define the business and its marketplace, and establish a strategic vision

Phase II

Set strategic objectives and performance targets expressed as the strategic mission

Phase III

Formulate a strategy to achieve the mission. Set performance milestones

Phase IV

Implement the strategic plan

Phase V

Evaluate performance and reformulate the plan and/or its implementation process

Re-examine as needed

Revise and reword, as neccessary

Reformulate as needed

Redefine the process, as needed

Review Phases IV-I, as needed

These three points lie at the heart of the Kaizen approach to customer care. They also underpin the strategic approach known as *relationship marketing*.

This brings into closer alignment product quality, customer service and corporate culture and concentrates their focus through the lens of (internal and external) marketing activity on:

- customer retention
- continuous customer contact
- product benefits
- a service emphasis
- satisfying customers' expectations
- making quality and improvement the personal responsibility and mission of each employee.

The product of relationship marketing is a passion for customers. This, of course, must be more than mere words (as I emphasized earlier, when discussing the 'emptiness' of many customer charters and service promises); the key success factors that will give substance – depth – to that passion include, for example:

- absolute clarity in what the company is, what it sells and to whom it sells
- uncompromising dedication to quality and real customer care
- inspirational and visible leadership
- listening to, measuring and responding to customers' needs and expectations
- cherishing front-line staff
- educating, informing, motivating and enabling all staff
- designing and implementing capable processes and systems
- managing resources productively
- learning, adapting and improving continuously by researching

and analyzing customer and market forces, and by having in place appropriate coping and recovery procedures (eg Kaizen's PDCA cycle).*

Throughout these Phases it is the responsibility of a company's executive team, senior managers and staff leaders to:

- maintain a clear focus on the vision, mission and strategy to prevent strategic drift
- reinforce strategic values through their personal conduct
- promote the company's objectives and goals internally
- facilitate any required behavioural changes
- promote the benefits of any paradigm shift.

In summary, managing the development of a strategy can be shown diagrammatically (*see* page 182).

2 DEVELOPING A KAIZEN CULTURE

The central premise of this book is that customer care based on and integral with a Kaizen cultural foundation will bring tangible benefits. However, the decision to introduce Kaizen – which must be a strategic decision taken and approved at the highest level in a company – will create repercussions felt at every level of the company. Some familiar organizational and managerial anchor points, which may have been taken for granted as self-evidently immovable for years, may have to be replaced by the new systems, style and process of Kaizen.

---

* Recovery strategies include getting better at the basics of service delivery. The *best* is providing added value as close to the point of customer purchase as possible; recognizing when things could go wrong and develop adequate coping procedures; measuring what is happening with customers' complaints; giving front-line staff the means and personal power to act quickly to redress faults; and recognizing what customers value when things do go wrong.

改

A Summary Model of the Elements of Strategic Management

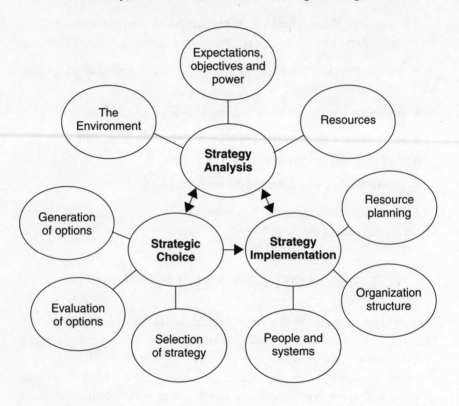

What makes a Company's Culture?

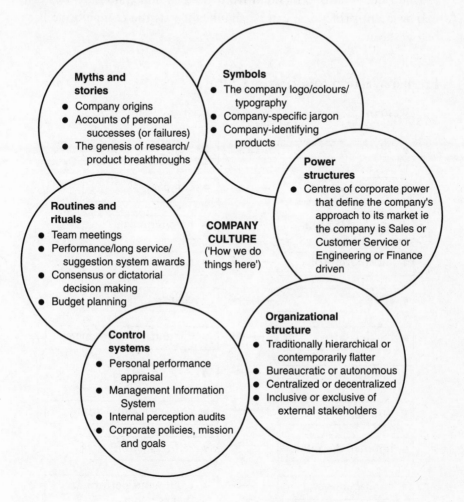

Myths and stories
- Company origins
- Accounts of personal successes (or failures)
- The genesis of research/ product breakthroughs

Symbols
- The company logo/colours/ typography
- Company-specific jargon
- Company-identifying products

Power structures
- Centres of corporate power that define the company's approach to its market ie the company is Sales or Customer Service or Engineering or Finance driven

Routines and rituals
- Team meetings
- Performance/long service/ suggestion system awards
- Consensus or dictatorial decision making
- Budget planning

COMPANY CULTURE
('How we do things here')

Control systems
- Personal performance appraisal
- Management Information System
- Internal perception audits
- Corporate policies, mission and goals

Organizational structure
- Traditionally hierarchical or contemporarily flatter
- Bureaucratic or autonomous
- Centralized or decentralized
- Inclusive or exclusive of external stakeholders

改

The change from a conventional Western organizational model to a Kaizen one, even one blended from Eastern and (familiar) Western management principles, can be significant – as the comparative lists below show.

From a Western to a Kaizen Culture

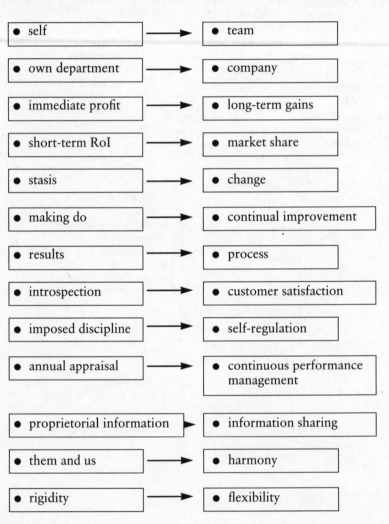

Western		Kaizen
• self	→	• team
• own department	→	• company
• immediate profit	→	• long-term gains
• short-term RoI	→	• market share
• stasis	→	• change
• making do	→	• continual improvement
• results	→	• process
• introspection	→	• customer satisfaction
• imposed discipline	→	• self-regulation
• annual appraisal	→	• continuous performance management
• proprietorial information	►	• information sharing
• them and us	→	• harmony
• rigidity	→	• flexibility

From Western Management to Kaizen Management

Western   *Kaizen*

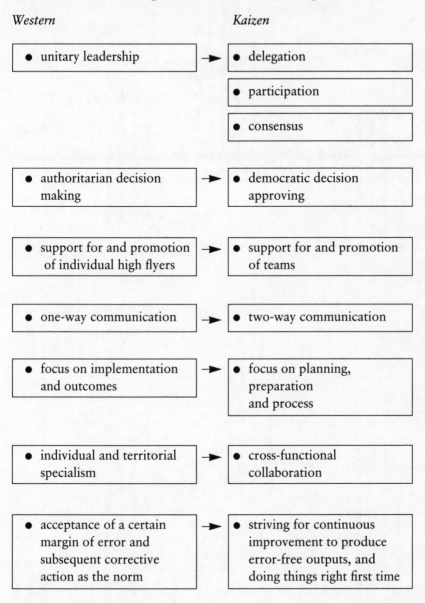

改

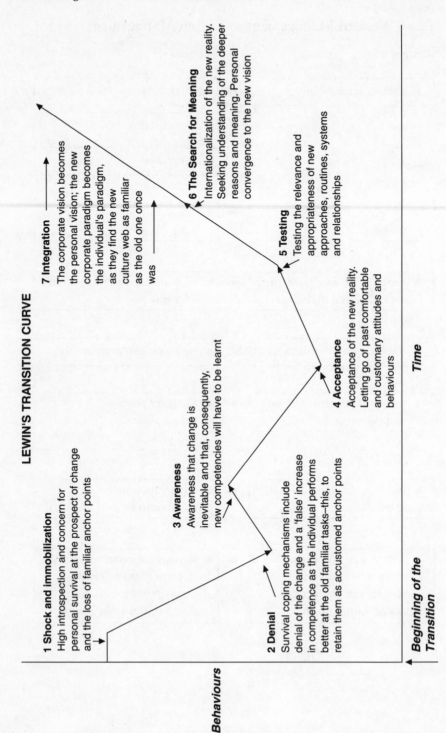

LEWIN'S TRANSITION CURVE

1 Shock and immobilization
High introspection and concern for personal survival at the prospect of change and the loss of familiar anchor points

2 Denial
Survival coping mechanisms include denial of the change and a 'false' increase in competence as the individual performs better at the old familiar tasks—this, to retain them as accustomed anchor points

3 Awareness
Awareness that change is inevitable and that, consequently, new competencies will have to be learnt

4 Acceptance
Acceptance of the new reality. Letting go of past comfortable and customary attitudes and behaviours

5 Testing
Testing the relevance and appropriateness of new approaches, routines, systems and relationships

6 The Search for Meaning
Internalization of the new reality. Seeking understanding of the deeper reasons and meaning. Personal convergence to the new vision

7 Integration
The corporate vision becomes the personal vision; the new corporate paradigm becomes the individual's paradigm, as they find the new culture web as familiar as the old one once was

Behaviours

Beginning of the Transition

Time

It is vital that a transition from purely Western to Western-plus-Kaizen be controlled closely and managed well, not only to prevent strategic drift and consequent dilution of the new vision but also to reassure existing power brokers who can fear loss of formal position or informal influence. Blocks to change can exist at both group (for example, Union) and individual (for example, long-serving employee) levels. Changing old attitudes can be achieved by either coercion and manipulation or, more positively and constructively, through information, education and training. But it is important to be fully aware of how employees can react to changes to their company's culture or strategic focus; the American psychologist Kurt Lewin, for example, has said that individuals can respond to significant changes to their familiar anchor points or environment by changing their behaviour in a chaim reaction as shown in the diagram on page 188.

It is the act of switching from a Western culture and management style to accepting and living according to new Kaizen values that Sir Colin Marshall referred to, when he spoke of culture change being meaningless if it is not 'built on a firm base of truly altered value frameworks.'

How then, can a company introduce these new Kaizen values?

The Route to Introducing Kaizen Values

Before embarking on any phase it is essential that the aims of the change are clear: why do you want to do this? What do you want to get out of it?

改

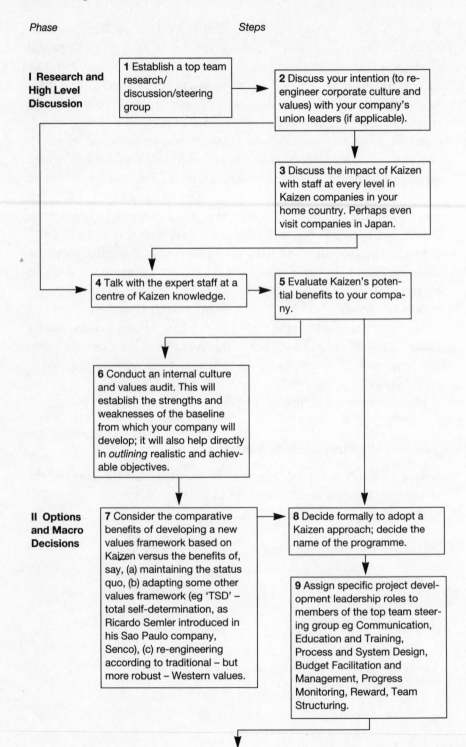

Phase   Steps

I Research and High Level Discussion

1 Establish a top team research/discussion/steering group

2 Discuss your intention (to re-engineer corporate culture and values) with your company's union leaders (if applicable).

3 Discuss the impact of Kaizen with staff at every level in Kaizen companies in your home country. Perhaps even visit companies in Japan.

4 Talk with the expert staff at a centre of Kaizen knowledge.

5 Evaluate Kaizen's potential benefits to your company.

6 Conduct an internal culture and values audit. This will establish the strengths and weaknesses of the baseline from which your company will develop; it will also help directly in *outlining* realistic and achievable objectives.

II Options and Macro Decisions

7 Consider the comparative benefits of developing a new values framework based on Kaizen versus the benefits of, say, (a) maintaining the status quo, (b) adapting some other values framework (eg 'TSD' – total self-determination, as Ricardo Semler introduced in his Sao Paulo company, Senco), (c) re-engineering according to traditional – but more robust – Western values.

8 Decide formally to adopt a Kaizen approach; decide the name of the programme.

9 Assign specific project development leadership roles to members of the top team steering group eg Communication, Education and Training, Process and System Design, Budget Facilitation and Management, Progress Monitoring, Reward, Team Structuring.

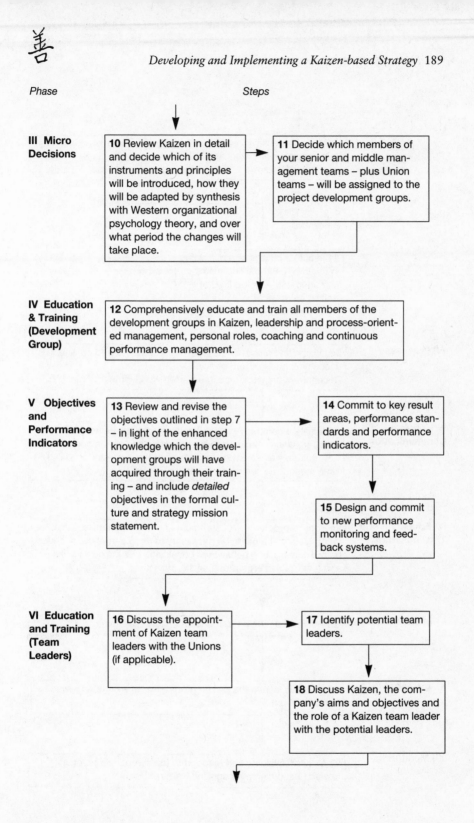

Phase   Steps

III Micro Decisions

10 Review Kaizen in detail and decide which of its instruments and principles will be introduced, how they will be adapted by synthesis with Western organizational psychology theory, and over what period the changes will take place.

11 Decide which members of your senior and middle management teams – plus Union teams – will be assigned to the project development groups.

IV Education & Training (Development Group)

12 Comprehensively educate and train all members of the development groups in Kaizen, leadership and process-oriented management, personal roles, coaching and continuous performance management.

V Objectives and Performance Indicators

13 Review and revise the objectives outlined in step 7 – in light of the enhanced knowledge which the development groups will have acquired through their training – and include *detailed* objectives in the formal culture and strategy mission statement.

14 Commit to key result areas, performance standards and performance indicators.

15 Design and commit to new performance monitoring and feedback systems.

VI Education and Training (Team Leaders)

16 Discuss the appointment of Kaizen team leaders with the Unions (if applicable).

17 Identify potential team leaders.

18 Discuss Kaizen, the company's aims and objectives and the role of a Kaizen team leader with the potential leaders.

改

Phase   Steps

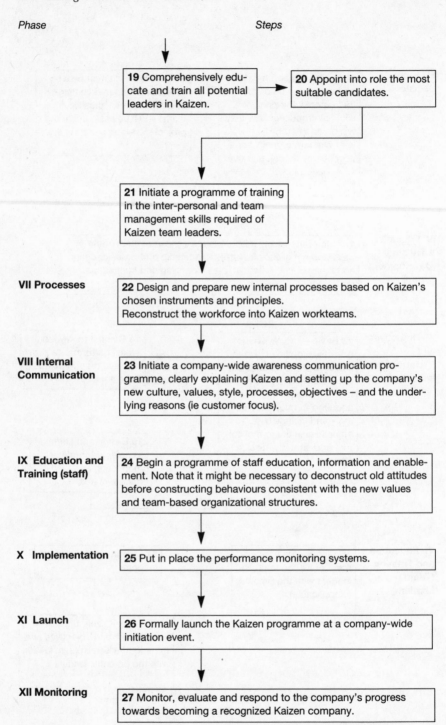

19 Comprehensively educate and train all potential leaders in Kaizen. → **20** Appoint into role the most suitable candidates.

21 Initiate a programme of training in the inter-personal and team management skills required of Kaizen team leaders.

VII Processes

22 Design and prepare new internal processes based on Kaizen's chosen instruments and principles.
Reconstruct the workforce into Kaizen workteams.

VIII Internal Communication

23 Initiate a company-wide awareness communication programme, clearly explaining Kaizen and setting up the company's new culture, values, style, processes, objectives – and the underlying reasons (ie customer focus).

IX Education and Training (staff)

24 Begin a programme of staff education, information and enablement. Note that it might be necessary to deconstruct old attitudes before constructing behaviours consistent with the new values and team-based organizational structures.

X   Implementation

25 Put in place the performance monitoring systems.

XI Launch

26 Formally launch the Kaizen programme at a company-wide initiation event.

XII Monitoring

27 Monitor, evaluate and respond to the company's progress towards becoming a recognized Kaizen company.

Amplified Explanation

Phase I. Steps 1 to 6

Kaizen *must* be led from the top, not just in the sense of project leadership but also behaviourally. The irreducible dependence on the managing director and members of the top team to be Kaizen role models is absolute for a successful change from conventional Western practices. This group of executives must, therefore, fully understand Kaizen and be prepared to sell its benefits to unions and staff, and steer its introduction down through their organization. Large-scale research – at home and, if possible, in Japan – is vital, as is discussion with a centre of Kaizen knowledge whose consultants can help tailor the transformation process to suit the current baseline (determined by a values audit) on the one hand and the (at this stage) outline objectives on the other.

It goes without saying that, instituting a paradigm shift needs constant hands-on management: it is not, of course, like changing a railway timetable when, at a certain hour on a particular day a controller throws a switch and all traces of the old schedule are replaced by the new; a new culture will take time – often years – to fully replace the old, and during the transition both will be perceptible, until the *ancien régime* has completely drained out of the system under the propelling influence of the new. This is especially true if the new culture/values framework is perceived to be inherently 'alien'. British Airway's culture change programme (now a decade old) is still being refined; Unipart's adoption of Kaizen has, in the same sense, only just begun.

Phase II. Steps 7 to 9

Step 7 is optional; the point of taking it is to be able to reassure doubters and waiverers that, compared to alternative values frameworks Kaizen is justifiably the most appropriate and beneficial philosophy to pursue.

Having decided formally to adopt Kaizen, perhaps under a different name (Step 8), the members of the top team steering-group can take on specific project development responsibilities. The seven development roles shown in Step 9 are only the prime roles – others might be necessary according to the company's current state and its goals. In any event, the project leaders can now invest their intellectual capital in small-scale research on the detail and minutiae of Kaizen in preparation for ...

Phase III. Steps 10 to 11

Of Kaizen's many instruments, only a few are *directly* relevant to a customer-care programme. (This is not strictly true, as the end purpose of them all is to enhance customer satisfaction; but some, for example SPC, are designed directly to improve production processes more than relationship or personal involvement processes.) The project leaders should concentrate their in-detail review on these and, at the same time, consider how to blend Western organizational and management theory into the Kaizen framework. Also, an overall time plan must be designed.

But note that Kaizen's instruments and principles should be introduced in a measured way – perhaps only one or two at a time, on a drip-feed basis. To introduce Kaizen wholesale will likely scare more than stimulate.

At this point the intention to adopt Kaizen can be made more clear to senior and middle managers, by bringing them into the groundwork reviews, discussions and planning and assigning individuals to the project-development groups. Union leaders, too, if applicable, should be included fully at this step (Step 11) to ensure that, first, they have no cause to feel that Kaizen is being imposed and, second, they have equal opportunity to share the transition and thus own the final product on behalf of and with their members.

Phase IV. Step 12

Sufficient groundwork will have been completed by this phase for the education and training, which the development groups can now receive, to write into a set of personal competencies. However, as a major part of the foundation of understanding could have been *self*-developed up to this point (if a consultancy has not been involved throughout) it could be incomplete. If this is the case it will be a worthwhile decision to invest in a structured awareness and skills programme from Kaizen experts at Step 12.

Phase V. Steps 13 to 15

This phase is the watershed phase in the transition from old to new values: the steps up to this phase have been fundamental, these and those to come are creational. The broad 'directional' objectives outlined at Step 6 can now be reviewed and refined to produce firm and formalized 'achievement' objectives, summarized in a corporate mission and values statement.

At the same time, the key result areas, standards of performance and the performance indicators that will be the signposts (or mile markers) along the route to fulfilment of the achievement objectives can be established. Similarly, new performance monitoring systems can be designed.

Phase VI. Steps 16 to 21

It will be remembered how vital team leaders are to the enablement of employees. They have a high-profile role in every Kaizen company. Their qualities as motivators, trainers, communicators, leaders, counsellors, psychologists, resource managers, chairmen, are much more important than their age or task skills and experience. For all these reasons choosing the right team leaders is crucial to the fulfilment of the achievement objectives. Hence the time and care implied by the six steps in this phase.

However, it might not be wholly necessary to follow these six steps precisely. For example, Steps 17 to 19 could be included in a combined briefing, training and assessment centre, from which suitable candidates can be selected and appointed (Step 20). These people can then go on to developmental training to prepare them specifically for their team responsibilities (Step 21).

Phase VII. Step 22

Trained team leaders are now available to be included in the design of the processes with which they must work. Their ideas concerning

改

workforce reconstruction will underscore and support their feeling of personal responsibility for the emergent teams.

Phase VIII. Step 23

At this point the Kaizen initiative can be rolled out to the entire workforce. Every channel of communication should be used: group briefings, videos, help desks, newsletters, all-point notice board bulletins and posters, explanatory booklets and, most definitely, 'management by walking around' (MBWA) by the managing director, members of the development groups, team leaders and union officers. Of greatest prominence in all communication must be the new corporate Kaizen mission and values.

Phase IX. Step 24

Staff training can now begin. This must be conducted by the team leaders. However, it might still be necessary, despite the communication and help activities at Step 23, to deconstruct die-hard attitudes and behaviours before educating staff in the new beliefs and processes: these must not be contaminated by abandoned past practices.

Phase X. Step 25

The new performance monitoring systems can now be put in place, just prior to …

Phase XI. Step 26

Launching the Kaizen programme on a specific date.

Phase XII. Step 27

Finally, progress must be monitored to ensure convergence of behaviours with the values and aims, and to allow reinforcement coaching and corrective action to be applied with point-like precision. It is worth reiterating that introducing a new culture and values framework will not be completed overnight, nor over one week, month or year. The transition must be nurtured and refined over many years. Kaizen is not something which can be put in place and left. It needs to be improved continuously and become a natural part of the organization's development.

———

I recognize how relatively easy and linearly sequential the steps in the schematic makes the transition from Western to Western-plus-Eastern appear to be; I also acknowledge that the process might not be as formulaic nor as fast in actuality as the schematic suggests. For example, there will inevitably be a great deal of overlap as different project-development groups work on their assignments; some steps could take longer to complete than others, thus delaying the completion of a phase; and some steps *will* take longer than others due to their possible complexity (eg Step 22) or the sheer number of employees who, for example, must be informed (Step 23) or educated and trained (Step 24). Nevertheless, such problems can be overcome – a detailed Critical Path Analysis (or fishbone diagram) are necessary planning tools that will help managers anticipate and cope with the dynamics of culture change. The overriding determinators of success, though, are goal focus, a commitment to succeed, communication (that is, keeping the workforce informed), motivation (that is, ensuring the workforce wants to achieve the objectives as much as the top team does), momentum, (that is, maintaining the pace and direction of change not only during what could be a period of many months but also afterwards to ensure *review and improvement* are continuous elements of the new culture), and training to ensure that when the Kaizen initiative 'goes live' it is launched into a receptive, educated and willing environment that nurtures and sustains growth of the new values.

The key is to introduce Kaizen in the Kaizen way, little by little: get one improvement accepted and cemented into the new values framework before introducing another. Build each improvement/change step on the one before.

改

> ## UNIPART
>
> Had John Neill heeded City advice in the late 1980s he would have stripped Unipart of its saleable assets and turned the rump of the company into a simple retail and distribution operation. Instead, he confounded critics of the company by keeping Unipart intact and inviting Kaizen experts from Honda to help him 'build a company which understood customers' needs and served them better than anybody else.' He 'decided to build a different type of business despite the industrial chaos that surrounded us.' He says, 'Honda taught us that work isn't about moving exhausts down a production line, but about controlling waste, cutting costs and more efficient production. This involves liaising with suppliers and eliminating any waste for mutual advantage.' In 1993, Unipart's Premier Exhaust Systems plant in Coventry was voted Britain's Best Factory.
>
> As Neill said, work is not just about shifting metal, the quality of relationships is critically important. He sees suppliers and customers as Unipart stakeholders – a group which also includes the company's shareholders, employees and the community. He believes that companies should be judged less by such typical City measures as RoI or EPS and more by the strength of stakeholder relationships.[21]
>
> John Neill involved and involves his company's stakeholders in the culture change he steered through Unipart, hence the mutuality of the strategic partnerships today.
>
> Source: *Sunday Telegraph*

Companies do not need to take a visibly theoretical approach to the introduction of new customer-care initiatives. A UK Building Society, for example, has made simplicity a key part of its management of customer relations.

NATIONWIDE BUILDING SOCIETY

Like many financial institutions, Nationwide Building Society is keen to differentiate itself from its competition. In an effort to do this, the Society two years ago took a long, hard look at its operations. Its own research and independent data soon indicated that differentiation would come through quality of service to its customers.

One of the major challenges was how to win over the hearts and minds of staff to the cultural change necessary to improve customer service. To do this a process of simulated experiences for teams to test drive were created. This became known as the Customer Connection process. Through this experience, staff could discover for themselves ways in which they could improve how they think and act together as suppliers and customers, working towards a common goal.

The Society felt it was important to keep everything in simple, everyday language and to avoid buzzwords such as 'vision' and 'mission.' Words such as 'here' (where we are now) and 'there' (where we want to get to) are commonly used.

Another key feature of the programme has been the identification of 'early adopters' – people in the company who act as advocates and influence their followers by example and word-of-mouth. The Society believes that if an idea is 'cascaded' through all levels of staff in the hierarchy, a tremendous amount of unnecessary energy is expended battling at each level, and the attempt to change the culture can be derailed. By using 'early adopters' as internal champions, there is a much better chance that people will be positively influenced.

改

I will now turn to the development of the right customer-care attitudes, and I will follow the same presentation: first, a broad schematic; second, an amplified explanation.

3 DEVELOPING A CUSTOMER-CARE APPROACH

The opening paragraph of the Press Release announcing the winners of the 1994 *Sunday Times*/Unisys *Customer Champion Awards* reads: 'It happens a million times a day – that vital moment when a customer makes a decision. The relationship between organizations, private and public sector, and their customers whether they be consumers, passengers, business customers, tax payers, patients, readers or subscribers, is becoming more and more crucial. Businesses are having to fight harder and harder to win, keep and satisfy an increasingly demanding audience.'

How, then, can a company create the right internal attitudes to achieve the status and recognition that wins customer-care awards?

The Route to Building Customer Care

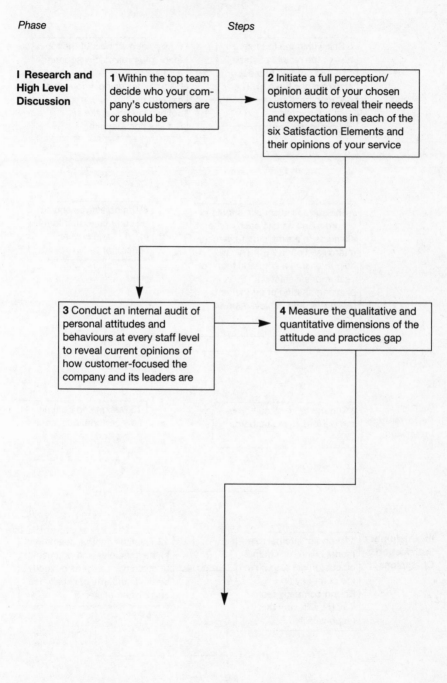

Phase   *Steps*

I Research and High Level Discussion

1 Within the top team decide who your company's customers are or should be

2 Initiate a full perception/opinion audit of your chosen customers to reveal their needs and expectations in each of the six Satisfaction Elements and their opinions of your service

3 Conduct an internal audit of personal attitudes and behaviours at every staff level to reveal current opinions of how customer-focused the company and its leaders are

4 Measure the qualitative and quantitative dimensions of the attitude and practices gap

改

Phase   *Steps*

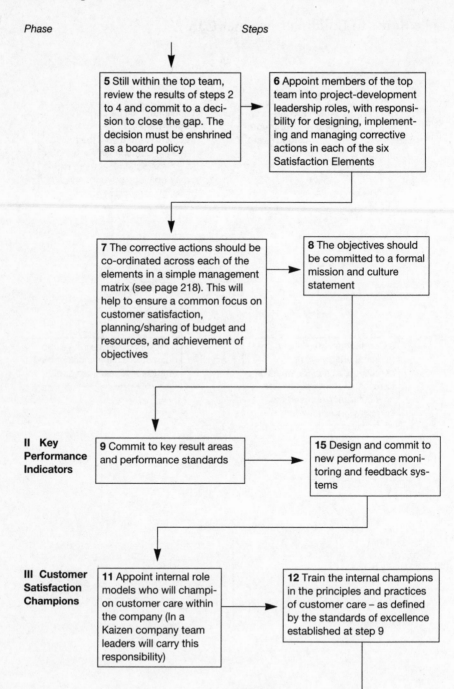

5 Still within the top team, review the results of steps 2 to 4 and commit to a decision to close the gap. The decision must be enshrined as a board policy

6 Appoint members of the top team into project-development leadership roles, with responsibility for designing, implementing and managing corrective actions in each of the six Satisfaction Elements

7 The corrective actions should be co-ordinated across each of the elements in a simple management matrix (see page 218). This will help to ensure a common focus on customer satisfaction, planning/sharing of budget and resources, and achievement of objectives

8 The objectives should be committed to a formal mission and culture statement

II Key Performance Indicators

9 Commit to key result areas and performance standards

15 Design and commit to new performance monitoring and feedback systems

III Customer Satisfaction Champions

11 Appoint internal role models who will champion customer care within the company (In a Kaizen company team leaders will carry this responsibility)

12 Train the internal champions in the principles and practices of customer care – as defined by the standards of excellence established at step 9

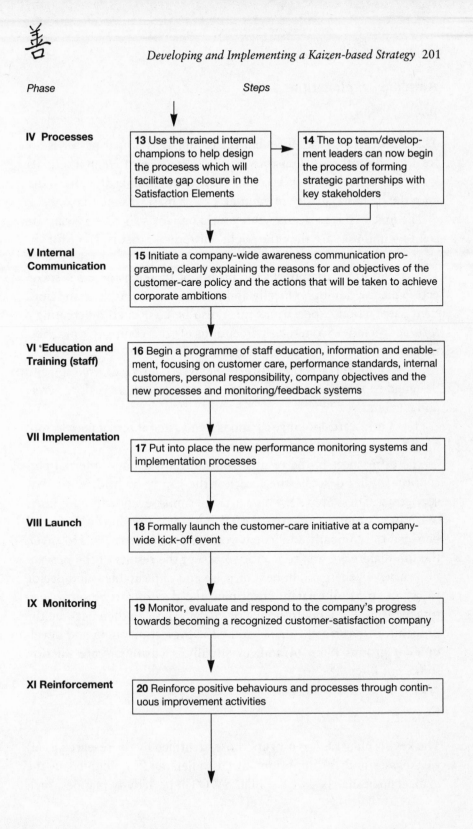

Phase

Steps

IV Processes

13 Use the trained internal champions to help design the procesess which will facilitate gap closure in the Satisfaction Elements

14 The top team/development leaders can now begin the process of forming strategic partnerships with key stakeholders

V Internal Communication

15 Initiate a company-wide awareness communication programme, clearly explaining the reasons for and objectives of the customer-care policy and the actions that will be taken to achieve corporate ambitions

VI Education and Training (staff)

16 Begin a programme of staff education, information and enablement, focusing on customer care, performance standards, internal customers, personal responsibility, company objectives and the new processes and monitoring/feedback systems

VII Implementation

17 Put into place the new performance monitoring systems and implementation processes

VIII Launch

18 Formally launch the customer-care initiative at a company-wide kick-off event

IX Monitoring

19 Monitor, evaluate and respond to the company's progress towards becoming a recognized customer-satisfaction company

XI Reinforcement

20 Reinforce positive behaviours and processes through continuous improvement activities

改

Amplified explanation

Phase I. Steps 1 to 8

This is a crucial phase, for what the company is preparing for is not for itself but others, its customers. In a service-sensitive marketplace where product, brand and company differentiation is difficult to discern the defining quality of genuine care is markedly significant.

The first step is to decide who your company sells to – or wants to sell to – and ask, are they the 'right' customers; that is, right for the strategy?

It is important to confirm the profile of these customers – socio-economically, demographically and in needs terms. At the same time, their satisfaction expectations must also be confirmed by creating a satisfaction index from their perceptions of your company's practices in each of the six Satisfaction Elements.

Steps 1 and 2 are therefore exclusively outward-looking, and designed to make knowledge of the chosen customers real, concrete and current.

Step 3 is inward-looking. Its aim is to measure internal perceptions of the company's service orientation.

The differences in the results from the external and internal perception studies describe the facets of the gap to be bridged by new service activities (Step 4). These activities must eventually fuse inner and outer opinions to create total harmony ('organizational fit') between the company and its environment and customers. However, the top team have first to decide to accept the results of the perception surveys – these might be a surprise and unpalatable – and decide to act (Step 5), ultimately enshrining the decision to be more customer-focused in a board policy or vision. This can then become the progenitor of a strategy managed by the project planning and development groups (Step 6) and, eventually, a customer-care mission statement (Step 8).

Phase II. Steps 9 to 10

The key result areas (Step 9) are those identified by the research as (a) weaknesses and (b) important to customers and highlighted in the management matrix – or a similar SWOT-type activity planner, such as the one designed and used by Fort Sanders Hospital Group (see page 133).

It is the particular performance standards which are chosen (also Step 9) that will help define 'the unique qualities of self'; that is, the identifying characteristics of the company's culture and values. Marks and Spencer's customer-service standards, for example, are the tangible and commonly-experienced symbols of its culture and help distinguish this store from, say, British Home Stores or the Next chain of clothing and household shops. (Note that the standards will also influence recruitment policy.)

Which standards any one company chooses will be decided by what its customers want – their expectations – and the generic standards of excellence, such as those listed on pages 55–64. The point to remember is that performance standards must cover both *actions*, eg answering a telephone within a certain number of seconds, responding to customers' correspondence within so many working days, managing complaints via sympathetic routines, as well as the *quality* of those actions, eg *how* an in-bound call or letter is answered, the *style* of complaint handling, the informed responsibility and responsiveness displayed by staff.

Observance of the standards must be monitored, and the measurements fed back to the staff involved, via the monitoring and feedback systems designed at Step 10. But the measurements and feedback of them will be pointless if their meaning – their consequences – are not followed through and used as developmental drivers. This is the basis of a learning organization, of a Kaizen company – the cyclical foundation of its continual improvement in service quality and response to customers' needs and expectations. It is this specific concept which underwrites the point that the design and implementation of a customer-care programme is *not* a one-shot affair: customer care is a 'living' discipline – once launched it must be nurtured, adapted and developed continuously, if only for the reasons that its target population – customers – are adapting and developing their demands and expectations, and supplier/customer relationships are dynamic. If the standards of a care programme are not reinforced quantitatively and qualitatively it will fail in time.

改

Phase III. Steps 11 to 12

The responsibility of the internal service champions is to take the strategic objectives and standards of a care programme down to every tactical level and each employee in the company. They are the prime internal conduits of the company's service culture. They must translate the inanimate policy into animate behaviours and conduct. They must ensure that every employee acknowledges and accepts a personal mission to support their company's focus on customer satisfaction. Clearly, therefore, they must be *enabled* as role models. They must consciously understand the deep meaning of what the company is doing and its values framework; this requires them to go beyond merely observing the structural logic or formality of being customer responsive (which results in customer 'processing' born of a fixated stimulus – response attitude such as, 'Thank you. Have a nice day now!' rather than genuine customer 'care'.) They must be trained, motivated and encouraged to develop creative (but realistic) personal and administrative responses and given responsibility to pass on their insight and skill to their teams. They are responsible, too, for seeking out and implementing feedback. And for this, communication from the top to them is vital.

In Kaizen companies, these responsibilities are fulfilled by team leaders.

Phase IV. Steps 13 to 14

Having determined the service objectives, designed the visible signs (the standards) of the objectives and identified and trained the service champions, the processes can be designed (Step 13). These must answer the question, how will the service mission be implemented? For example, how will:

- technology be used?
- internal communication channels be improved to serve customers better?
- customer research be conducted, analyzed and the results fed into the internal service chain?
- performance be measured and upgraded against the standards?

- staff be involved in regular team training and information meetings?

- good performance be recognized and rewarded?

- new ideas (for service improvement) be encouraged, captured and reviewed?

- complaints be managed, and the lessons learnt and incorporated in future behaviours/processes?

- partnerships be invited and cemented?

At Step 14 the company can start to consider seriously its future trading relationships with customers and suppliers, and how its own growing awareness, changing image and developing maturity can be reflected in more trusting and confident relationships with key stakeholders.

Phase V. Step 15 and Phase VI. Step 16

These two steps should be directly sequential with no time delay, the foundation training for all in core customer-care competencies following an intensive and comprehensive internal marketing campaign to raise awareness and interest.

The communication and training activities should inherently raise development expectations; that is, the company's staff should *come to expect* more and more information and more education not only as a consequence of the precedents set by these initial activities but also because the 'fragility' of a customer-care programme in its early months demands constant bolstering to ensure it becomes integral with the corporate culture and second nature to the staff. The company must therefore be prepared – in terms of budget, material resources and time – to follow up these two steps quickly, frequently and regularly.

Phase VII. Step 17

The final step prior to programme launch is to put in place the new processes and systems.

改

Phase VIII. Step 18

The launch should be a managed and motivating event, a definitive statement that clearly signals the start of the company's pursuit of a new customer-satisfaction mission.

The launch can even, of course, include suppliers and key customers: they are as intimately involved in the ultimate goal as are the company's own staff.

Phase IX. Step 19

Monitoring will be by team leaders' personal observation of their people at work, more formal internal opinion research, and external customer (and supplier) research. The speed and quality of response is important, to remedy weaknesses and prove to customers that *their* needs and perceptions are being noted and used to shape the company's offering across each of the six Satisfaction Elements.

Phase X. Step 20

Kaizen means continuous and gradual improvement. It is as important to reinforce employees' confidence, motivation and competence through knowledge and skills training and coaching as it is to improve manufacturing processes or the standards of customer-care performance themselves. Learning from what customers think of how their complaints have been handled is just one example of using field data to stimulate an improvement exercise; team meetings to review how well the concept of internal customers is being accepted is an example of an improvement activity stimulated by personal anecdote and first-hand experience. In any event, the capacity of customers and of prolonged concentration on providing total satisfaction to erode commitment and skill should never be underestimated; for this reason reinforcement is vital to maintaining objectivity, focus and momentum.

ICI PAINTS*

Many of the principles in this process were adopted by ICI Paint's managing director Herman Scopes back in 1988. At that time ICI Paints were one of ten 'super league' leaders in paint worldwide, but were facing increased competition both in the UK and Europe. A policy decision was taken that the way to beat this challenge was to meet customers' needs better than the competition.

A major customer-care initiative, 'Focus on the Customer' was initiated. Prime consideration within the process was given to the concept of servicing internal customers. This was presented graphically as each employee being a member of a relay team, using the baton to represent service. The management team considered it vital that there was genuine 'buy in' from members of staff, that the initiative was not seen just as 'flavour of the month'. Research was undertaken to convince employees of the need for change. Initially this was done internally to give everyone an opportunity to suggest ways of improving the business, and to air any grievances they might have. A personalized letter from the CEO accompanied the research questionnaire. Next, market research was undertaken with customers to compare ICI Paints' performance, products, and service against that from its major competitors. The findings of this research were then provided openly to all employees.

To launch the whole 'focus on the customer' programme the company organised a multimedia road show, which brought to every employee broad factual information about the paint industry worldwide, competitive threats, and the findings of both the internal and external research projects. Employees then heard detailed research findings specific to their own department. Management presented the quality and service strategy to staff. Tom Peters, the management guru, gave a lecture to an audience of approximately 300 managers, and a video of his presentation was produced for wider distribution.

Focus groups were formed to take forward ideas that emerged from the market research surveys, and many devices were used to compound the message and develop ideas. These included regular updates of programme progress displayed on notice boards, competitions such as 'if I were CEO for the day' designed to stimulate

▶

改

▶

innovatory ideas, and branding everything from notepaper to mouse pads with the programme's logo to keep message reinforcement high.

Every couple of years in the UK the programme is handed over to a new management team, to revitalize ideas and build on the ground work from the past. Market research, both internal and external, is undertaken annually and this has indicated a marked change for the better in employees' attitudes, co-operation, and commitment. During one year, for example, there were 180 employee focus groups operating on a voluntary basis, often during their own time. More than 850 practical ideas as to how the business could be improved have been logged. Some ideas needed capital expenditure, but the vast majority could be implemented easily by the department concerned or by co-operation between departments. The programme was designed to improve quality of operation and performance, but due to increased efficiency there has been a saving of some £500,000 after implementing just a few dozen of the suggested improvements.

Initiatives such as those taken at ICI Paints are not limited to the private sector, as the case history below illustrates.

SOUTH THAMES BLOOD TRANSFUSION SERVICE

When Belinda Phipps and a new management team took over the running of the South Thames Blood Transfusion Service in 1991, both effeciency and morale were low. Since then, efficiency has been lifted to levels that are widely admired elsewhere in the National Health Service.

Changes have been made as part of a campaign entitled '560 Brains are Better than One', through which all staff have been consulted, involved and empowered. Improvements have ranged from relatively minor changes, for example using good lighting and plants to enliven the reception area, to more complicated ones, such as changes in working arrangements so that blood can be reprocessed at night, rather than the day after collection.

Underpinning the changes has been a new focus on customers. When the new management team began work, they discovered that staff were confused as to whether the Service's customers were the donors who provided the blood or the patients who received it. A purpose statement, now hanging in the reception area, makes clear that the Service's core job is to ensure that hospitals can always be supplied with whatever blood products they require. The purpose statement reads: 'To help save and improve the lives of patients, with services and products provided through the generosity of donors.'

Putting together the three core strands – developing a strategy, developing a Kaizen culture and developing a customer-care approach, plus the concept of learning organizations – gives a coherent scheme leading to a new model for a Kaizen approach to customer care:

改

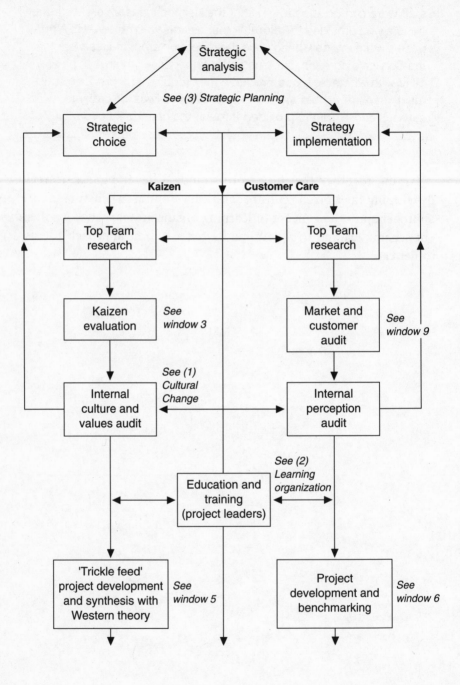

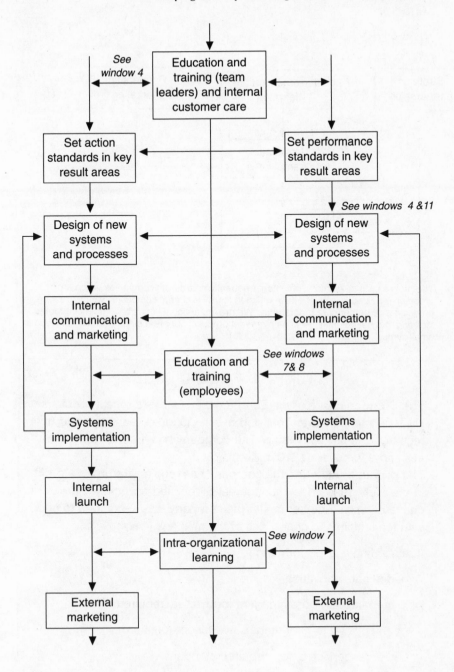

改

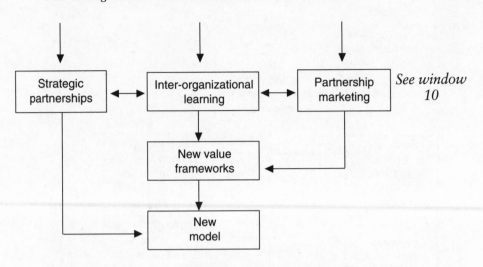

See window 10

The process will take time: a comment frequently heard from companies which are embracing Kaizen is, 'We still have much to learn', and from companies which are pursuing a customer-care programme, 'We are improving all the time' – both comments implying that neither initiative is an overnight process; but great strides can be achieved in small steps.

A UK FOOD MANUFACTURER

The Company: One of the Europe Japan Centre's recent clients is a UK food manufacturer, founded over a hundred years ago and until recently in family ownership. The company has around 120 employees and a turnover of £10 million.

The problem: Although the company has regularly returned a profit, in the early 1990s new management identified several key areas of concern which together meant the company was ill-equiped to cope with the anticipated challenges of the next few years:

- static financial performance

- pedestrian innovation

- ill-prepared for more stringent food safety requirements

- poorly placed to beat more powerful competition

- customer service below required standard

- poor industrial relations, characterized by many petty grievances

- a hierarchical and autocratic management style

The process of change – Stage 1

Management made the decison that if the company was to survive and prosper, attention had to be focused in two areas:

- investment in the facility
- 'turning the people round' and involving them in the business.

This highly summarized study focuses on the second of these priorities.

From the start the new management made the decision that they had to break down the 'them and us' culture; they needed to introduce a new culture of confidence, open government and involvement. They decided to do this gradually, but systematically.

The first steps included:

- *developing an open door policy*: managers made themselves widely available to all employees, regularly spent time on the shop floor, committed themselves to giving as many direct answers as possible, gave out more information about the business to all employees, etc. As a result, people in different positions in the company began to understand more about the business, more about other people's problems and skills, and more about their own role in the business.

- *bringing together people from various departments to resolve issues*: rather than launching straight into a team approach to everything, *ad hoc* groups were set up to examine specific issues, for example quality and supply. In this way, people began to see the value of working together in groups to solve problems, and some of the barriers that had existed between different departments began to come down.

- *skills training*: new skills, particularly computer training, had been neglected, so staff were encouraged to volunteer for training. As a growing number of staff became proficient in using computers, other more-fearful members of staff were encouraged to volunteer so that, finally, very few people remained computer illiterate.

The process of change – Stage 2

As the climate in the company began to change, management decided to move the programme into its next stage: much greater involvement of all employees. This included a number of major steps:

►

改

- *instigating regular company meetings*: the company is small enough for everyone to gather together in one large room, so twice-yearly meetings were introduced, at which the senior managers spoke about the company's past and future performance and staff were encouraged to ask questions. Initial criticisms that there was too much management talking, that the meetings were too short and the information too statistical were dealt with at later meetings.
- *choosing team leaders and setting up workteams*: the company considered it vital that more decisions and responsibility should be devolved to people on the production line and at other points where problems arise. Rather than always seeking authority from their supervisors, and they in their turn seeking authority from their managers, employees would operate in autonomous workteams and be trained and encouraged to resolve problems themselves. Team leaders were chosen and trained in people management.
- *introducing a Kaizen programme*: again, the policy of employee involvement led management to think employees should spend time trying to improve their performance and that of their team, to look to future problems – not only to fire-fight. For this, Kaizen training and the introduction of a Kaizen approach were considered vital.

The process of change – role of the Europe Japan Centre
The Europe Japan Centre was invited to help the organization and to reinforce management's determination to introduce change. EJC were brought in with specific aims:

- to help the entire workforce understand the changes and to gain their support and enthusiasm
- to work with senior management on maintaining the momentum for cultural change
- to help senior management develop a mission statement and corporate vision
- to assist in the introduction of Kaizen
- to improve the performance of team leaders and help create real teams, rather than 'accidental' work groups.

Before beginning the programme Europe Japan Centre interviewed a cross-section of people throughout the company to establish areas of strength and concern. The programme was then devised specifically to take account of these findings.

Throughout the training and development programme, EJC was very much aware that one of the main underlying aims was to try and instill confidence in people, to encourage them to ask questions and challenge current practice – not just upwards but sideways, too. As people's knowledge about the business grew, and as their skills developed, so too did their confidence. Management's confidence in their abilities and acknowledgement of their importance to the organization further reinforced the growing mood of open power sharing.

The whole process of awareness and competency development extended over many months. By the end of the period, many positive changes had been introduced:

- regular team meetings were initiated. 20 minutes a week, within work time, is allowed for discussion
- team leaders began to adapt to their new role of encouraging their team, praising achievements and boosting performance, rather than merely handing down orders
- teams began to function in a more focused way, identifying and beginning to solve problems and look for improvements
- business knowledge had increased: daily sales figures were posted on notice boards; the annual sales plan was available for any interested employee to take away and read
- team members took on more personal responsibility, for example, for attendance records, performance logging, suggesting and carrying out improvements to the working environment, and to processes
- multiskilling began in several parts of the factory; and concurrently, management spent some time working on the shop floor
- a cross-functional group was set up to examine ways of specifically improving quality
- a cross-functional group was set up to visit a supplier with whom the company was having problems; as a result, a new direct link between the supplier and the manufacturer's quality-monitoring team was established
- performance measuring systems were established by team leaders as well as by the senior management team, so that the progress of the various initiatives could be measured

The process of change – Stage 3
Training and development has only just begun within the programme

▶

改

described above. As the company progresses, new areas need to be dealt with (the need for a more sophisticated appraisal systems, the need to redefine team leaders' jobs as team members become more proficient, ways of maintaining motivation, momentum, etc.). The company regards the development of its people as a continuous aim and annually sets new standards for achievement and involvement.

The Results

During the year since EJC began to work with the company, a number of tangible results have emerged:

- appreciably higher output
- £100,000 saving on the direct labour budget
- a 30 per cent increase in service levels.

Less immediately tangible, but nonetheless important, results include:

- a happier, more committed and more responsible workforce
- closer relationships with and higher standards from suppliers
- an atmosphere of continuous improvement
- a greater dedication to quality and customer service.

A simple Management Matrix to Co-ordinate Actions and Resources Across the Six Satisfaction Elements

An example of the matrix being used by a particular company is shown overleaf. In the example, the company has ticked the areas which their own research has identifed as being areas of weakness. For example, the research has identifed that After-sales Satisfaction could be improved by focusing on four areas (those marked in the columns – training, enablement, selling and premises). Training has also been identified as a focus for corrective action in three other areas – Product, Sales and Culture.

By using the matrix, the company can co-ordinate Training and After-sales as part of their total plan to improve customer care.

改

Focus for Corrective Action / Satisfaction Elements	Product	Sales	After-sales	Location	Time	Culture
People Communication						✓
Training	✓*	✓	✓			✓
Motivation						
Enablement			✓			
Recruitment						
Reward	✓					
Systems Information systems						
Market Research	✓	✓				
Marketing	✓					
Selling		✓	✓			
Business Admin.					✓	✓
Financial						
Order Processing		✓		✓		✓
Manufacturing	✓					
Packaging						
Distribution	✓					
Style Management						
Relationships						
Culture		✓			✓	✓
Structure Premises			✓			
Resources	✓					
Stakeholders						

Summary

- A fundamental shift in an organization's culture must be underpinned by a clear and communicated vision of the organization's new values framework, to eliminate arbitrary and capricious actions causing the organization to lose its way.

- The transformation must be *spearheaded*, it should not be advanced on a *broad* front that can dilute management control and intimidate employees by the sheer magnitude of the approaching change.

- Accountability must be allocated to 'project-development groups', each responsible for a specific aspect of the transformation process, and within each group to particular members tasked with completing precise project activities.

- Intentions must be supported by visible leadership by the managing director. The power of his or her presence – symbolic, reassuring, tangible – should never be undervalued.

- Involve as many people as possible in planning and executing the transformation. The greater the number of employees (from every level) who feel they have been consulted in deciding what the new values should be and how they should be introduced, the greater will be ownership of them and the commitment to accepting new work practices.

- Ensure that the measurement and control systems support the new values; in other words, it could cause considerable confusion if, having emphasized customer-care values, employees' performance is still measured against previous and now superseded standards. Performance must be measured and rewarded with respect to the new requirements.

- Don't 'try and eat the whole elephant'; in other words break down the development and implementation of a new culture and a customer-care initiative into manageable process steps, which can be controlled and introduced precisely. And be selective: choose which Kaizen instruments and customer-care standards *you* want to introduce into your company, and over what timescale, and work towards that goal never taking your eye off the ball – off your strategic mission.

11

AVOIDING
THE
PITFALLS
AND
MAINTAINING
THE
MOMENTUM

改

THE PITFALLS AND PROBLEMS

I have written elsewhere in this book that neither Kaizen nor 'the Japanese way' are wholly models of virtue even in Japan; at bottom, both have weaknesses, as well as great strengths. What many Western organizations are trying to do is take some of the strengths, and combine them with their own strong points. One initial stumbling block for companies thinking of introducing Kaizen may be the word itself.

And yet, so much of TQM – which we embrace enthusiastically – is rooted in Kaizen, if we did but know it. (In truth, as I explained in the Chapters on Kaizen and Kaizen's Instruments, a great part of the Japanese way in manufacturing is actually based on the original ideas and teachings of two Americans). But it does not matter that TQM users do not understand the origin of its behaviours and practices; indeed, because TQM is itself becoming something of a clichéd term many TQM programmes are launched under disguising titles. To make initiatives their own, many companies have invented their own names for TQM or Kaizen. These include:

- *Continuous Improvement*
- *Working Together*
- *Our Contribution Counts*
- *Total Involvement*
- *Focus on Quality*
- *Focus on Customers*

- *Putting (The) Customer(s) First*
- *560 Brains are Better than One*
- *Customer 1st*
- *We All Make The Difference*

If wrapping up Kaizen ideas in a more palatable coating helps, so much the better; no one will mind, least of all the Japanese who themselves are past masters at Japanizing things Western!

What are the other common pitfalls that can compromise the smooth introduction of a Kaizen approach to customer care?

Overcoming Middle Management Resistance

As we have seen, a great deal of the power, authority and autonomy exercised by Western middle managers is invested in team leaders in Kaizen companies. Naturally, middle managers can feel threatened that their role will be eliminated. This need not be the case. Their *traditional* role will change, but there is still a need in a Kaizen environment for 'middle managers'. The change involves them releasing day-to-day operational, or tactical, responsibilities to team leaders, and taking on more strategic responsibilities – those of managing, monitoring and controlling a number of teams' activities to ensure convergence with their own planned strategies. These strategies will in turn be managed and co-ordinated by more senior managers who, in their turn, will respond to the corporate strategies and ideas handed down to them from company executives.

Thus many middle managers who have been through the process of introducing Kaizen into their companies have, first, needed reassurance that Kaizen does not spell automatic redundancy, and second, required training to help them change their management perspective and skills from tactical to strategic, from functional to business process. In this they will implicity take on the responsibility for championing and driving the Kaizen approach.

In some cases, the introduction of Kaizen, like the introduction of other flatter management structures, has, however, led to redundancies. Clearly it is in the interests of all parties for management to be as open as possible about the results of change and to make all possible efforts to find other employment, for example in subsidiaries, associated companies or new business.

改

Overcoming Union Worries and Fears

Again, a union's role in a company that adopts Kaizen will ideally change from the traditional one to a less confrontational one. Their *focus* – their prime interest – may still be the welfare of their members, but in an open culture where employees are positively encouraged to share information, take responsibility, participate in decision-making processes, accept ownership of their own development, collaborate in cross-department ventures and share more equally in company rewards, some of the factors over which unions and management previously fought are eliminated. As a consequence, employees may voluntarily reject union representation and the company may prefer either to have single union presence or none at all, on the presumption that the need for union activity no longer exists.

Throughout Europe, unions have expressed worries about the introduction of Japanese working practices, voicing criticisms such as:

- employees are encouraged to work themselves out of a job
- older workers may be edged out in favour of younger, fitter ones
- employees need to work harder but have no greater rewards.

Some of these fears may be overcome in a traditional Japanese situation (where lifetime employment has so far been guaranteed for male employees in large corporations, for example, and where the rewards for higher profitability are more equally spread across the whole company than in the UK or the USA), but are not necessarily able to be overcome in the same way in the West. Managers therefore need to consider very carefully how they are going to handle these issues, and to look at the whole package of rewards and benefits they are offering staff.

Several companies in the UK have introduced specific measures to try and overcome some of these fears. The most popular are guarantees of employment (eg Rover, Rolls Royce). Other ideas include work at Nissan UK on designing facilities ergonomically (for ease of working) and the introduction of a physiotherapist, offering treatment in company time as a benefit for employees and also advising on ways of working to relieve physical stress.

Overcoming Disappointment at Never Achieving Perfection

Two aspects of the Kaizen approach to customer care militate against achieving perfection. The first is that customers' needs and expectations are dynamic: what is wanted today can be declined tomorrow – whatever amounts to 'perfection' now can be 'suspect' later; and as soon as expectations are met the threshold rises. Thus, as customers themselves set the standards of excellence and these are forever becoming more stringent, companies will rarely achieve perfection: it is, by definition, an unobtainable.

The second aspect lies within Kaizen itself. In Kaizen, a standard is transitory: it should last for only as long as it takes an individual or a team to find an improvement that betters it. In Kaizen, too, a standard is never seen as a target, for achieving a target can induce a feeling of success and that therefore there is nothing more to achieve. By definition, again, perfection is an unobtainable: no product or process or relationship is ever so ideal in a Kaizen company that it defeats even some small attention (to design, manufacture, cost control, waste reduction, etc.) to improve it. Today's 'perfect' washing machine, camera, stereo system, car, photocopier, earth mover, watch will quickly become obsolete if employees are *allowed to believe* they have achieved perfection. Customers' fickle demands makes perfection an illusion (or at the most, merely momentary).

Clearly, if the search for an ideal never ceases the team leaders and managers in a Kaizen company have a plain responsibility to motivate, communicate, lead by personal example and make time to be with their people. Employees tend to respond well if they see the difference their efforts are making to the company's performance, and if they can share in those gains.

Overcoming a Lack of Time

Maintenance and reinforcement beyond the initial foundation inputs are crucial to ensuring there is no cultural slip back to the pre-Kaizen/customer-focus way of operating. It should never be underestimated how much resource and time it will take to change employees' thinking and behaviour permanently: the shift in personal beliefs and conduct expected of employees in the change to Kaizen

改

and the new focus on customers will likely demand the same whole-sale education and support as that given to maturing students; and in the same way that preparing students for any major test is a process of building their knowledge and confidence step-on-step, so it should be with employees – they will benefit from a trickle-feed approach to their training and development, each step – each success in personal change – taking them further and further away from the old values and inter-personal behaviours and nearer to the new.

Clearly, such personal transformation will not be the result of education and training *per se* alone: psychological support, personal coaching, role modelling and establishing teams as the new foundation units of corporate life all play an equally important part in propelling staff forwards and making the new cultural model a compelling motivator.

None of this will happen by accident, nor just because the managing director has said it will. All levels of management – including the managing director and the top team – and all team leaders must be seen, through their own wholehearted and personal commitment to the Kaizen approach to customer care, to be leading the process of change and reinforcement of the change. This is not a light burden to carry. If the managing director and his or her senior managers are to be role models, which they must be, they should initially each devote at least 40 per cent of their working week to being with their employees – on the shop floor, in team meetings, at communication events, in the offices, on training courses – and a further 20 per cent of their time with customers and suppliers – on the telephone and in face-to-face meetings, to market the company's new vision, find out what customers want and develop partnership relationships with them and the suppliers. This can require a tremendous shift in their work patterns: if 60 per cent of their time during the maintenance and reinforcement phase (which could last from one to three years) is to be spent with employees and customers, then the work that they once did during this time will have to be managed in another way, either by someone else – which means delegating it – or through better organization of their time and tasks. Either case represents a golden opportunity for senior managers to demonstrate publicly their observance of the Kaizen way: in the former case, delegation demonstrates open sharing and trust in the empowerment given to the delegate and in the latter case, better personal-time management demonstrates a desire to improve personal efficiency by reducing wasted time (plus effort and resources). But again, managers might not be good delegators or time organizers just because they are managers: they too might benefit from skills training to equip them for their new work processes – and their redefined roles.

Maintaining the Momentum

The prime objective during this continuous phase of development is to integrate continuous improvement into the core-business strategy and corporate culture, and overcome any tendency to see Kaizen as a 'bolt-on' initiative.

How?

The most powerful way is to compile a *fully integrated* business plan that merges customer-care aims, the ownership of quality, corporate culture and the responsibility of suppliers to work in partnership to meet those customers' aims. The plan thus becomes the written expression of the permanence of Kaizen and the three-way partnership that will characterize the way in which the company will manage itself and its conduct.

A plan on its own will not maintain the momentum adequately. First, the plan must be communicated to all employees in a language which *they* will understand, and using all internal communication channels to draw everyone closer to the corporate culture. Second, suppliers also must be drawn into that culture – it, the culture, must become the arbiter determining the quality of partnership values and action. Third, customers must be informed of what the company is trying to achieve; but, and this is a big 'but', the company and its supplier partners must be ready to deliver: you probably remember British Railways' 'We're Getting There' campaign aimed at its customers; the trouble was, BR never did get there – nothing appeared to change or improve; promises were never, or rarely, delivered and the organization was castigated for hiding lack of action behind self-congratulatory, but ultimately hollow PR.

In support of the plan, employees must be continuously motivated to accept and observe the importance of the new culture, and that their participation is critical to the success of the customer-facing approach. In other words, they bear a responsibility for ensuring that the initiative *does* deliver and does not die on the gallows of empty rhetoric. Managers and team leaders must be prepared to invest time, money and effort in developing the attitudinal maturity to acknowledge and accept personal ownership of the concept, the practice and the goals.

In addition, the key qualities required – flexibility, participation and innovation – must be recognized and rewarded via a positive reinforcement system that is meaningful to employees and consistent with Kaizen principles and objectives – a Kaizen-style suggestion system serves this purpose well. But remember, in Kaizen companies the primary (though not the sole) beneficiaries of suggestion-system rewards are teams; teams, therefore, must be continuously supported to encourage autonomy, self-direction and ownership of responsibilities – obviously, without compromising the drive for and integrity of the company's business objectives.

In its turn, this means that team leaders must be equipped with the leadership skills required to maximize team effectiveness (and, with an eye very much on the Kaizen way, to team *efficiency*.) They must also be trained to understand and communicate the core-business objectives, and trained in the inter-personal skills that will enable them to use their authority to measure performance against those objectives and take remedial actions with confidence and expertise.

Using an approach to performance measurement based on the concept of internal customers, will help everyone understand the part they play in the service chain. In its turn, this will help employees and teams convert performance measurements into process improvements through which they can express ownership of the continuous improvement cycle.

In summary, then, we can say that the process of maintaining the momentum of a Kaizen approach to customer care is one of:

Leadership

Leadership is everything. It is the single most important activity that will transform the Kaizen concept into a practical working tool suitable for Western business, for through the example, inspiration, motivation, dedication and communication of leaders a company and its employees will make the transition to a continuous improvement company.

Persistence

Chasing perfection is a fruitless pursuit, but striving continuously to improve not only pays dividends it is essential to remaining competitive, for the more a company does for its customers the more they will want and expect. Improving customer service is not a case of only achieving a certain satisfaction rating and then resting back on the laurels. In Kaizen companies, today's rating, like any standard, is simple a new base line from which the company can progress to the next level.

> Companies have evolved various ways of keeping the importance of customers always in employees' minds. At Ricoh Techno Net, posters on office walls ask 'Are customers satisfied?' and remind employees of their conversations with the company president (*see* page 60). One company in the USA has allegedly had 'Remember our customers' woven into its carpets!

Communication

This is one of the elements that keeps everyone – employees, customers and suppliers – focused on a common goal. The most effective communication is direct contact.

> When the Royal Bank of Scotland introduced a Kaizen approach, they recognized that communication was one of the most vital elements. The bank ensures that service quality is continually at the forefront through regular communications, which are designed to be attractive and readable. All communications are aimed at particular target audiences, rather than a 'blunderbuss' approach.

Involvement

This is another co-ordinating element, that springs from effective communication and strong leadership. Needless to say, every employee must be encouraged to become involved in customer service, given opportunities to do so, and expected to accept a personal responsibility to contribute positively to service activities, process and deliverables.

Training

As Marion Loveday wrote in her November 1993 article in *Best Practice* magazine, '*A Guide to Better Service*', 'Provide everyone in the organization with the appropriate education and training in quality tools and techniques; for example, flow charting, cause-and-effect and Pareto diagrams, problem-solving, and brainstorming. This enables them to make a meaningful contribution to improving customer service and handling customer complaints.' I would add to the list of training requirements, inter-personal skills, communication skills (telephone techniques, presentation techniques, report writing), team working, task-and-time management and creativity skills.

> As part of its customer relations training, Midland Electricity's HR department has produced a series of videos, 'As others see us'. Employees see exactly how customers view the company, whether their contact is on the telephone, on the doorstep or in the street.

Measurement

Measuring every process in a Kaizen company against its objectives and its customers' expectations is not a control activity imposed by management to police performance; rather, it is a self-assessment activity performed willingly and completed honestly by each employee to help them identify improvement gaps and their contribution to improving service along the entire service chain. The results are made public to employees and customers so that everyone is able to see and comment on progress. Ownership of a customer-service initiative by employees, customers and suppliers – the members of the three-way partnership- is thus strengthened.

At the Forte Harvester restaurant chain, employees now work in teams to do their own recruitment, devise their own publicity stunts and track their own sales targets. One immediately measurable result has been a significantly lower employee turnover – and that in a sector notorious for high absenteeism and staff turnover.

Satisfying employees

Measuring everything contributes to employee satisfaction – *provided that poor performance does not lead to a blame culture but, rather, to learning and improvement opportunities.* This is the basis of a learning organization, in which employees feel valued, trusted, motivated and, importantly, enabled to perform and *enabled to correct their own mistakes.*

Recognition and reward

Recognition means a team leader or manager saying 'thank you' to an employee; this requires them to be with their employees more frequently than not simply to notice positive contributions and give praise on the spot and at the time. Rewards can be financial or non-financial; as I stated earlier, Japanese companies are adopting the Western system of merit or performance pay and bonuses, but a certificate, a public citation, a mention in the company newsletter, a photograph on a company noticeboard are all equally powerful ways of rewarding (and encouraging) high performance.

Listening to customers

Fortunately, the days of companies producing what they want to and telling customers that this is what they can have are rapidly being replaced by a genuine desire to produce what *customers* want, need and value. Knowing what this is means listening to what they are saying and responding appropriately. But given the speed with which customers' needs can change, market and customer research must, like improvements, be continuous. There is a point here that is very important: companies should not simply respond to their larger customers; fleet buyers, for example, are motor manufacturers' largest customers, but what they have found is that private buyers do not always like mass-produced 'Euromobiles'; what private motorists want is a more personalized car that is individual to them, whilst retaining the build quality, price, service intervals and guarantees designed-in for fleet users. Customization packs have thus become big business for all vehicle producers.

> Milliken, the US Modular carpet company, have made listening to customers a vital part of their 'opportunities for improvement' activities. Not only does an important part of staff training focus on listening for 'things we could learn from'; more surprisingly, at dealer conferences the company picks out for praise those customers who have complained the most!

Knowing customers

There are two ways by which a company can know its customers: first, as a set of demographic and socio-economic statistics and second, as real people who have and will express their emotions. Statistics will help define a service *strategy;* emotions will define how customers want to be treated at a personal level. Both ways of knowing customers are necessary.

I want to end by quoting a case study at some length. To me, what Tom Hay, the Managing Director at Bard UK Ltd, has achieved encapsulates much of what this book is about.

> ### BARD UK Ltd
>
> Bard's parent company is in the USA. Its style represents what we in the UK think of as typically American: dynamic, results-oriented and responsive to shareholders. By contrast, Bard UK was struggling to meet its targets when Tom Hay was appointed Managing Director.
>
> Tom's approach to business was at that time unique in Bard. He focused more on employees than the products or other, external, stakeholders. His first (unwritten) function was to establish his credibility as a change agent, rather than as an operational director only. And so began a seven-year period of slow but unremitting change

and development within the company, focusing on the company culture, values, structure, internal communication, personal relationships, attitudes, behaviours and the quality of its responsiveness to customers. As Tom says, 'Nothing I did was revolutionary; it was many small steps, single and in combination, that gradually pulled the company together and turned it around.'

In the last four years business has doubled and in 1994 Bard UK won the award for most outstanding performance of all international divisions within the Bard Group.

How did Tom Hay achieve this success?

His first step was to look at how 'user friendly' Bard was as an organization to buy from. Having a very broad range of products, the customer would often be purchasing different parts of the range from various purchasing points around the country. To introduce the concept of 'one stop shopping', Tom merged the customer-service teams into one, based in Crawley, thus centralizing the buying process.

It is common to find in organizations that are under threat – due, for example, to poor performance – a great deal of introspection, fairly solid psychologically – protective walls put up by employees around themselves or their departments, a lack of effective internal communication, and a measure of defensiveness. Tom realized that he had to win his employees' trust, before the inter-departmental barriers would be dismantled and harmony could replace suspicion and individualism.

The Customer Care department at Bard, as so often in organizations, was often 'dumped on', and unappreciated for their contribution to the business. To change employees' perception of the department, including, one might add, the care teams' own perception, Tom commissioned me to develop a customer-care programme in stand-alone manual format so that, over time a broad cross-section of staff in the organization could access the programme to become aware of customer-service issues. Tom specified that part of the programme should be personal developmental (in this instance assertiveness training was required). To break down a further barrier, when new product managers come on board they spend a week as part of their induction in the Customer Service department. Written into the product manager's job description is their responsibility to train the customer-care team in all new product developments.

▶

▶
In addition, he cross-trained the once separate product-based customer-care teams in each others' product ranges to create a single consolidated and unified team, any member of which can respond to any customer query that, now, comes into the company via a common enquiry-line gateway. Further, the customer-care team has been trained beyond its traditional service role to make each employee an 'account manager,' able to handle any order, service, complaint or query issue. As Tom says, 'We want to make it as easy as we can for customers to buy from us.'

Tom's vision did not stop at that horizon. He encouraged all non-management staff to attend regular brainstorming/creativity retreats, where not only were real problems debated but the feeling of being involved, of participating, of making a felt-contribution was strongly reinforced. It was in these sessions that Tom's focus on developing the 'soft' skills, what he calls 'the hardest skills of all' – inter-personal communication, giving feedback, leadership, team playing – paid dividends. The personal and departmental walls started to come down quickly once people learnt to differentiate between in-role and out-of-role personas, and once people realized that self-protective agendas were no longer required.

None of Tom's ideas or approaches is unique (he admits to plagiarizing any idea from anywhere if it helps him achieve his objectives and make his vision concrete). His ideas on team development, for example, are classic in their simplicity. He recreated teams from singleton employees based on the concept of the internal customer, on cross-functional responsibility for projects, and on delegation. But most of all on the idea that if teams are the building blocks of company structure they must be given the opportunity to exercise autonomy for decisions *and* for when decisions go wrong. Tom strives to achieve 'balance' in his teams; in other words, one person's weaknesses can be balanced by another's strengths. In this way the whole *team* is strong. Similarly, he recognizes that not every manager is a good administrator; the right secretarial support can bridge that skills weakness and allow the manager to exercise their true strengths. Again, a team has been created and balanced.

Bard UK's management team now plays a high-profile training and development role in the company. Each project team is mentored by a board member. This reflect's Tom's view that the function of good management is to challenge. And to be challenged – he has recently initiated 360° appraisals for board directors.

Tom is as equally insistent that his staff change and develop their attitudes as he is, so that his vision will be realized. If an employee is not prepared to observe internal customer relationships, 'even for 10 per cent of the time' he or she is asked to leave the company. He says that the company cannot afford a weak link in the chain: a weak link is disruptive, and sooner or later that weakness will work its way up the customer-service chain and effect the relationship with an external customer.

Now that Bard UK is so successful, it is being used as a model for other Bard divisions within the Group. But it has taken Tom Hay seven years to win recognition and reward; it has been his leadership, example, visibility, vision and persistence that has helped his top team and the company's employees stay the distance during a long transformation process.

Tom is now reasonably happy that Bard UK is internally satisfied and can offer external customer satisfaction. But the platform he has raised the company to today is just one step on a continuous improvement journey.

The future, as always, holds many uncertainties for companies and organizations throughout the world. As the pace of change accelerates, companies will need to be able to adapt quickly to new conditions, new working practices and new customer demands. In the customer-care area, new technology, the growth in teleworkers and home workers, for example, will pose new challenges to management.

Whatever processes are put in place, however, can only be as good as the people operating them. For this reason, if no other, the introduction of Kaizen-based attitudes and practices can only be beneficial. People who become used to the Kaizen way of thinking will be able to contribute more fully to your organization now: they will also be able to take it into the future with more enthusiasm and success than you may yet be able to imagine.

CASE STUDIES FEATURED IN
THIS BOOK

INDEX

改

Europe Japan Centre Training Programmes

All Europe Japan Centre programmes are individually tailored. Tuition is in small groups and is highly participative. The list below provides an indication of our main areas of expertise.

Awareness Sessions

Kaizen and Creativity
What is Kaizen and how can it be combined with Western creativity to form an unbeatable approach

Leadership of Tomorrow
The new role of senior management in creating world-class companies

Research and Consultancy

Our unique research programme (R&I) assesses the current state of your organization and begins the vital process of involving staff more fully

One-to-one sessions with senior managers provide advice and support on cultural change or particular aspects

Our consultants can work alongside your teams to advise on organizational and human resources changes

Seminars and Workshops to Develop Skills and Put Theory into Action

Implementing Kaizen

How to introduce a culture of continuous improvement, building on the strengths of your organization

From Managers to Leaders

How to inspire and develop your people

The Kaizen Approach to Customer Care

Using Kaizen to enhance your service to customers

Developing Effective Team Leaders

How team leaders can get the most from their teams in terms of productivity, efficiency and creativity

Creating Teams that Work

How to put together the right people, set guidelines, organize meetings and create results

Inter-team Co-operation

How to break down barriers between departments and work more efficiently across the whole organization

The Kaizen Toolbox

Practical tools and statistical techniques, from brainstorming to PDCA and Pareto analysis, to measure performance and improvements

The Kaizen Approach to Problem Solving

How to identify real problems, analyze their root causes and find creative solutions

Personal Development and Kaizen

Workshops to build the personal skills needed to embed Kaizen in the behaviour of everyone in your organization

Seminars and workshops can be arranged for all levels, from directors and senior managers to team leaders and team members.

Europe Japan Centre Services also include research on the Japanese market and Japan Briefings.

For further information or an informal meeting contact Pat Wellington or Barbara Wilson at:

The Europe Japan Centre,
Nash House, St. George Street, London W1R 9DE.
Tel: 0171–491 1791   Fax: 0171–491 4055